Sir Charles N

Sir William Francis Butler

Alpha Editions

This edition published in 2023

ISBN : 9789357935371

Design and Setting By
Alpha Editions
www.alphaedis.com
Email - info@alphaedis.com

Contents

CHAPTER I
THE HOME AT CELBRIDGE—FIRST COMMISSION

Ten miles west of Dublin, on the north bank of the Liffey, stands a village of a single street, called Celbridge. In times so remote that their record only survives in a name, some Christian hermit built here himself a cell for house, church, and tomb; a human settlement took root around the spot; deer-tracks widened into pathways; pathways broadened into roads; and at last a bridge spanned the neighbouring stream. The church and the bridge, two prominent land-marks on the road of civilisation, jointly named the place, and Kildrohid or "the church by the bridge" became henceforth a local habitation and a name, twelve hundred years later to be anglicised into Celbridge. To this village of Celbridge in the year 1785 came a family which had already made some stir in the world, and was destined to make more.

Colonel the Hon. George Napier and his wife Lady Sarah Lennox were two remarkable personages. The one a tall and majestic soldier, probably the finest specimen of military manhood then in the service of King George the Third; the other a lady of such beauty, wit, and grace that her fascination had induced the same King George to offer her all his heart and half his throne. Fate and politics marred this proposed romantic royal union, and the lovely Lady Sarah, after a most unhappy first marriage, became in 1777 the wife of Colonel George Napier, and in the following dozen years the mother of a large family, in whose veins ran the blood of a list of knights and kings and nobles sufficient to fill a peerage all to itself; for on one side the pedigree went back to the best of the old Scottish cavaliers—to Montrose, and the Napiers of Merchiston, and the Scotts of Thirlestane; and on the other it touched Bourbon, Stuart, and Medici, and half a dozen other famous sources. It would have been strange if from such parents and with such stock the nest which was built in Celbridge in 1785 did not send forth far-flying birds.

The house in which the Napiers took up their residence in this year stood a short distance from the western end of the village. It was a solid, square building of blue-gray limestone, three-storied and basemented, with many tall narrow windows in front and rear, and a hall door that looked north and was approached by arched steps spanning a wide stone area surrounding the basement; green level fields, with fences upon which grew trees and large bushes, spread around the house to north and west, and over the tops of oak and beeches to the south a long line of blue hills lay upon the horizon. Looking south towards these hills the eye saw first a terrace and garden, then a roadway partly screened by trees, and beyond the road the grounds of Marley Abbey sloping to the Liffey, holding within them still the flower-beds and laurel hedges amid which Vanessa spent the last sorrow-clouded years of her life. But to the boys up in the third-story nursery, looking out in the winter evenings to snowy Kippure or purple Sleve-rhue, the loves and wrongs of poor Vanessa mattered little. What did matter to them, however—and mattered so much that through a thousand scenes of future death and danger they never forgot it—was, that there stood a certain old larch tree in the corner of the pleasure-ground where the peacocks fluttered up to roost as the sun went down beyond the westmost Wicklow hill-top, and that there was a thick clump of Portugal laurels and old hollies where stares, or starlings as they call them in England, came in flocks at nightfall, and sundry other trees and clumps in which blackbirds with very yellow winter beaks flew in the dusk, sounding the weirdest and wildest cries, and cocked their fan-spread tails when they lighted on the sward where the holly and arbutus berries lay so thick.

When Colonel Napier settled at Celbridge he was still in his prime, a man formed both in mind and body to conquer and direct in camp, court, or council; and yet, for all that, a failure as the world counts its prizes and blanks in the lottery of life. He had recently returned from the American War, where he had served with distinction. He had filled important offices abroad and at home, and by right of intellect and connection might look forward almost with certainty to high military command, but he had one fatal bar against success in the career of arms, as that noble profession was practised in the reign of George the Third and for a good many years after—he was in political opinion intensely liberal and intensely outspoken. The phrase "political opinion" is perhaps misleading. Colonel Napier's liberalism was neither a party cry nor a prejudice. It sprang from a profound love of justice, an equally fixed hatred of oppression, and a wide-reaching sympathy with human suffering that knew no distinction of caste or creed. The selection of Celbridge as the Napiers' family residence at this period was chiefly decided by the proximity of the village to the homes of Lady Sarah's two sisters—the Duchess of Leinster at Carton, and Lady Louisa Conolly at Castletown—indeed only the length of the village street separated the beautiful park of Castletown from the Napiers' home, and Castletown woods and waters were as free to the children's boyish sports and rambles as its saloons were open to them later on when the quick-running years of boyhood carried them into larger life. Whatever was beautiful and brilliant in Irish society—and there was much of both—then met in the Castletown drawing-rooms. They were to outward seeming pleasant years, those seventeen hundred and eighties and early nineties in Ireland. The society that met at Castletown formed a brilliant circle of orators, soldiers, wits, and statesmen, many of whose names still shine brightly through the intervening century. Grattan, Curran, Flood, Charlemont, the Ponsonbys, Parnell, the Matthews, and younger but not less interesting spirits were in the group too; the ill-fated Lord Edward Fitzgerald (first cousin to the Napier boys); young Robert Stewart, still an advanced Liberal,—not yet seeing that his road to fortune lay behind instead of before him; and there was another frequent guest at Castletown—a raw-boned, youthful ensign, generally disliked, much in debt to his Dublin tailor, but nevertheless regarded by Colonel Napier, at least, as a young man of promise, who, if fate gave him opportunity, would some day win fame as a soldier—one Ensign Wellesley, or, as he then wrote his name, Arthur Wesley.

When the Napier coach drove into Celbridge with the newly-arriving family in 1785, there was in it a very small boy, Charles by name, the eldest son of the handsome colonel and his beautiful wife—a small, delicate-looking child, who had been born at the Richmond residence in Whitehall just three years earlier. Two other children younger than Charles made up, with the due complement of nurses and boxes, an imposing cavalcade, and for days after the arrival baggage and books—these last not the least important items in the family future—continued to trundle through the village.

Twelve years go by; 1797 has come. Long ago—what an age in childhood seem these few flying years!—little Charles has made himself at home in a circle ever widening around the Celbridge nest. He has a fishing-rod, and the river east and west has been explored each year a longer distance. He has a pony, and the mountains to the south have given up their wonders to himself and his four-footed friend. And finally, grandest step of all in the boy's ladder, he has a gun, and the wood-pigeons of Castletown and the rabbits out in big fences to the west know him as one more enemy added to the long list of their foes.

And how about the more generally recognised factors of boy-training— school and schoolmaster? Well, in these matters we get a curious picture of army-training in that good old time when George the Third was King. At the age of twelve little Charlie Napier had been nominated to a pair of colours in His Majesty's Thirty-Third Regiment of Foot. War had broken out with France. Mr. Pitt was borrowing some fifty millions every year, and commissions in Horse, Foot, and Dragoons, in Hessian and Hanoverian Corps, in Scotch Fencibles and Irish Yeomanry and English Militia, were plentiful as blackberries in the Celbridge fields. But though Charles had on many occasions shown himself a little lad of big heart and steady courage in sundry encounters with fish, flesh, and fowl, he was still too young to fight a Frenchman; and besides, it was even then a canon of war that before you are fit to kill an enemy in the field you must be able to write a nice letter to him, and perchance to talk to him in his own language, and to draw little lines and tracings of the various emplacements and scarps and counter-scarps by which you propose to knock his cities about his ears, and otherwise blow him and his off the face of the earth. So, instead of proceeding with the Duke of York's army to Flanders, Charles was sent to Mr. Bagnel's school in Celbridge village. A very humble and unpretending scholastic institution was Mr. Bagnel's academy,—not much further removed from the hedge-school of the time than the single street of Celbridge was distant from the green hedges around it; and of a very mixed description were the numerous boys who gathered there to receive from Mr. Bagnel's mind, and frequently also from his hand, the instruction mental and physical which he deemed essential for their future guidance. The boys were chiefly the sons of Dublin merchants or local better-class farmers, and were, with the exception of the Napiers, all Roman Catholics. That Charles and his brothers George and William should soon become the leaders of the school, and the child-champions of its youthful democracy, was not to be wondered at. They represented to the other boys the three most taking and entrancing things of boy life—genius, courage, and strength. All three boys were plucky as eagles, but Charles was captain by reason of his superior intelligence; George was lieutenant on account of reckless daring; William was ensign because of immense strength; and all were beloved because they, the grandsons of a duke, were ever ready to uphold with the weapons of boyhood the rights and freedom of their Catholic comrades against the overbearing usurpations and tyrannies of a large neighbouring seminary, where the more favoured sons of Protestant ascendancy were being booked and birched.

At ten o'clock every morning the Napier boys proceeded up the village to school, and at three they came down the single street for home. Great was the commotion when this hour of breaking-up arrived; it was the event of the day for the villagers, and no wonder, for then a strange sight was often to be seen. There were pigs in Celbridge in these days, tall gaunt animals with wide flapping ears that hung over their eyes, and long legs that could gallop over the ground; and it is said that, mounted on the backs of those lean and agile hogs, the Napier boys were wont to career homeward with scholars and pig-owners following in wild pursuit.

"What a terrible training!" I think I hear some worthy parent or pedagogue exclaim, reading this deplorable incident. And yet it is not all so clear this matter of boy-training. Would not the guiding lights of Eton and Harrow and Rugby stand aghast at such companionship, such a scene as this hog-race down the village? Still, somehow or other, when I walk round Trafalgar Square or down Waterloo Place, I seem to miss these great centres of training in the statues of Nelson, Havelock, Franklin, Clyde, Gordon, Lawrence, Napier; and I see beyond the bronze or the marble the boy-hero at his village school—one at Foyle, another at Taunton, a third at Celbridge, a fourth at St. Ives, a fifth at Swanscombe—until I come to think it is not quite so certain that we know all about the matter. So too, when my mind turns to the subject of military teaching, and I compare the course of school-training Charles and William Napier received at the hands of Mr. Bagnel with our modern system of competitive cramming, I am forced to the conclusion that both these brilliant soldiers would have been ignominiously "plucked" for entrance to Sandhurst or Woolwich; nor does the outside and casual training which these boys underwent show with less disadvantage beside our modern system. How a professor of military history, for instance, would have scorned the tuition in the practice of war conveyed to Ensign Charles Napier by old Molly Dunne as she sat in her cottage porch of a summer evening telling the listening boys about her battles and sieges. She was the Celbridge carpenter's great-grandmother, and of prodigious age. She could tell her listeners how she had seen the last real lord of Celbridge ride forth to fight for his king, their own great-great-great-granduncle, at the Boyne, just one hundred years earlier, and how she had seen his body brought back to be laid in the old graveyard of Kildrohid, close to their own gateway. That was a long look back, but Molly's memory went further off still, for she could tell of wilder times of war and havoc; of how as a little child she had heard people speak of the red days at Drogheda and Wexford, when Cromwell imagined that he had found a final method of dealing with the Irish question. This wonderful old woman, who had seen more of actual war than had many of the generals by whose military knowledge and experience Mr. Pitt just at this moment fondly hoped he was going to stop the French Revolution, was said to be about one hundred and thirty years of age.

But Charles Napier and his brothers had the benefit of one outside teacher, the value of whose teaching to them it would not be easy to exaggerate; out of doors and indoors, on the river and the mountain, their father was their best school-master. From him Charles Napier learned a thousand lessons of truth and justice, of honour in arms, of simplicity in life, of steady purpose, of hatred for pomp and show and empty-headed pride, of pity for the poor, of sympathy with the oppressed, of fearless independence of character, which those who care to follow us through these pages will find growing in profusion along the pathway of his life, plants none of which ever withered from the moment they were planted in these youthful days, but many of which were only to blossom into full luxuriance in the autumn of existence. When full fifty years have passed by we shall find the lessons sown along the Liffey, and amid the Wicklow hills, bearing their rich harvest in distant scenes by the shores of mighty Eastern rivers and under the shadows of Himalayan mountains. It has been said that the house at Celbridge held large store of books, and it may be that in the library a copy of old Massinger was to be found, wherein, if the boys were not allowed promiscuously to read, they had read to them that wonderful picture of the real soldier which the dramatist drew so uselessly for the Cavaliers of his time, so terribly useful for their Roundhead enemies.

> If e'er my son
>
> Follow the war, tell him it is a school
>
> Where all the principles tending to honour
>
> Are taught, if truly follow'd; but for such
>
> As repair thither as a place in which
>
> They do presume they may with license practise
>
> Their lusts and riots, they shall never merit
>
> The noble name of soldiers. To dare boldly
>
> In a fair cause, and for their country's safety
>
> To run upon the cannon's mouth undaunted;
>
> To obey their leaders, and shun mutinies;
>
> To bear with patience the winter's cold
>
> And summer's scorching heat, and not to faint,
>
> When plenty of provision fails, with hunger,
>
> Are the essential parts make up a soldier—
>
> Not swearing, dice, or drinking.

At last the time came for Charles to quit home and go out by himself into the world. He had been an officer on that wonderful institution called the Irish Establishment since he was twelve years old, and now he must join the army; so, in the last year of the century, he takes his first flight on the Limerick coach, and arriving in that old city is installed as extra aide-de-camp to the general officer there commanding. He remains at Limerick for a year, where the usual subaltern officer's drill is duly passed through. He is very often in love; he rides, shoots, breaks his leg jumping a ditch, and altogether feels quite sure that he has thoroughly mastered the military art. Still among these inevitable incidents of a young soldier's existence we get a glimpse of the nature of the future man coming out clear and distinct. He and his brother George are out shooting; a snipe gets up, Charles fires and the bird drops, but a deep wide ditch intervenes, and in springing across this obstacle the boy falls and breaks his leg. It is a very bad fracture, and the bone is sticking out above the boot. His gun (a gift from his father) has fallen one way, he is lying another. First he draws himself near enough to recover the weapon, then he crawls on to where the snipe is lying, and then when his brother George has come up and is looking deadly pale at the protruding bone, the fallen sportsman cries cheerily out, "Yes, George, I've broken my leg, but I've got the snipe." They carry him home on a door, and for two months he is laid up with this shattered leg; but at eighteen a broken heart or leg is soon set right, and early in 1800 we find him impatient to be off to wider scenes of soldiering. He has been run very low by this accident, and his general—fearful for his aide-de-camp's life—has written to Colonel Napier, advising leave of absence and rest for the boy. Charles hears of this letter shortly after, and is highly indignant at his general's action. "I am sure," he writes to his father, "you will never consent to do anything of the sort" (to apply to the Commander-in-Chief for leave of absence), "which you must think, and which you may be certain I think, would be disgraceful and unbecoming the character of a British soldier. The general would not have done such a thing for himself, and could not have considered much when he proposed it for me." Just fifty years later we shall see the war-worn old veteran taking leave of the officers of India in words of advice and farewell couched in the same lofty spirit of military duty which is expressed in this boy's letter. And now the scene changes.

Early in 1801 Charles Napier mounts his little Irish cob and rides away from Limerick to begin the career which was to be carried through such stirring and varied scenes. He rode in a single day from Limerick to Celbridge, more than one hundred miles, on the same horse. We know nothing of that long day's ride, save the bare fact of its accomplishment; but it requires no effort of imagination to picture this ardent, impetuous boy pushing forward mile by mile, intent upon proving by the distance he would cover that despite what generals might write or doctors might say, he *was* fit for any fatigue or duty; and as the Irish hill-tops rose before him in fresh horizons we can fancy the horseman's mind cast far ahead of the most remote distance, fixed upon some scene of European or Egyptian battle, where the great deeds of war then startling all men by their splendid novelty were being enacted before a wondering world. For only a few months prior to the date of this long ride a great battle had been fought at Marengo in Italy, and the air was still ringing with its echoes; then had come the news of Hohenlinden, that terrible midnight struggle in the snow of the Black Forest. Never had the world witnessed such desperate valour; never had such marches been made, such daring combinations conceived, such colossal results achieved. A new world seemed to be opening before the soldier; and France, victorious for a second time over the vast forces of the European coalition, appeared to have given birth to conquerors before whose genius all bygone glory grew pale and doubtful.

And already, amid the constellation of command which the seven years' aggression of Europe against France had called forth from the great Revolution, one name shone with surpassing lustre. Beyond the Alps, amid scenes whose names seemed to concentrate and combine the traditions of Roman dominion with the most desperate struggles of medieval history, there had arisen a leader in the first flush of youthful manhood, before whom courage had been unavailing, discipline had become a reed, numbers had been brought to ruin, combination had been scattered, the strength of fortress had been pulled down, until the great empire whose name had been accepted as the symbol of military power in Europe, and whose history went back through one thousand years of martial glory, lay prostrate and vanquished at his feet.

CHAPTER II
EARLY SERVICE—THE PENINSULA

Poor, proud, and panting for opportunity of action, Napier began his military career at this wonderful epoch, only to find his aspirations for fame doomed to disappointment. Marengo came to scatter the slowly built combinations of Europe. The victor held out the olive branch to his enemies; his offer of peace, which had been so insultingly refused one year earlier, was now accepted, and the Treaty of Amiens put an end to hostilities which had lasted for nearly ten years. All Charles Napier's hopes of service were destroyed. For six years he was to wander aimlessly about the south of England in that most soul-rusting of all idlenesses—garrison life at home. "What can one do?" he wrote to his mother upon hearing of the peace. "My plan is to wait for a few months and then get into some foreign service. Sometimes my thought is to sell my commission and purchase one in Germany or elsewhere; but then my secret wish could not be fulfilled, which is to have high command with British soldiers—rather let me command Esquimaux than be a subaltern of Rifles forty years old." Meanwhile he set vigorously to work at his books and studies. Already at Celbridge he had read every hero-book or war-history he could lay his hands on; now he applies himself incessantly to study. "I quit the mess," he writes in November, 1801, "at five o'clock, and from that to ten o'clock gives me five hours more reading. There is a billiard-table; but feeling a growing fondness for it, and fearing to be drawn into play for money, I have not touched a cue lately." Yet with all this longing for fame, the heart of the boy is full of his home memories. "Nobody but myself," he writes to his sister, "had ever such a longing for home. I shall go mad if you don't come to England or I go to Ireland; my heart jumps when thinking of you all merry in the old way. This wishing for home makes me gad about in a wild way; for melancholy seizes me when alone in a cold barrack-room, and I cannot read with thoughts busy in Kildare Street. I should like to go to London and stay with Emily [another sister], but I am too poor. I have no coloured clothes, and they are expensive to buy. My horse also is costly and must be sold; very sorry, for he is the dearest little wicked black devil you ever saw, and so pretty." But though this poor hard-up subaltern cannot afford to purchase plain clothes, and has to sell his dearly prized horse, he can find money to do a kind act to a friend. He is writing to his mother, that ever-ready listener to all his troubles and his joys.

> *January 1st, 1801.*—Happy New Year and many of them to my dearest mother. Now to ask a favour *not* to be told to

dad unless you think there will be no inconvenience to him. Cameron [a brother officer] has been in a very disagreeable situation for some time about family affairs. Several things have happened to put him to enormous expense, and he intends borrowing money from the Jews, which must do him much mischief in the end, though he will have a very good property when of age. Now if my father has not drawn the £100 of forage money belonging to me which Armitt has had these eight months, to repay the money you advanced, can he spare it for Cameron? You know the Comptroller [his father] as well as I do, and if you showed him the letter at once he would do the thing to oblige me, when perhaps it was troublesome. Cameron has not the least idea of this matter.

A very beautiful letter for all concerned—father, mother, son, and friend— and worth many long pages of description. Then he falls in love, is very miserable, goes to London, sees several of his rich relations, finds out he cannot afford fine life, and comes back again to his books and his dreams. The regiment is now at Shorncliffe. The colonel, a type of warrior at that time and for years later peculiar to our service, lived much at Carlton House and seldom saw his soldiers, who, groaning under a well-nigh intolerable discipline, were left to the mercy of the second in command. The picture we get of the result is a curious one. "*Shorncliffe, December, 1802.*—We are going on here as badly as need be. Two or three men desert every night, and not recruits either. The hospital is full of rheumatic patients and men with colds and coughs, caught from standing long on damp ground and being kept in mizzling rains for hours without moving."

Enough to damp a less ardent spirit must have been this barrack-room warfare, so delightful to so many excellent persons who imagine that a uniform coat makes a soldier. At last a slight change for the better came to Napier. A relation, General Fox, was made Commander-in-Chief in Ireland, and to Dublin went Charles as aide-de-camp. Through this move we get an inventory of his kit, which is suggestive of many things. He is writing to his mother: "You talk of magazines of clothes," he says; "why, I have no clothes but those on my back. I have indeed too many books—above thirty volumes; but books and clothes all go into two trunks." How the modern staff-man would shudder at the list of uniform which follows. "Nothing of mine, except linen, will do for an aide-de-camp. My pantaloons are green, and I have only one pair; my jacket, twice turned; a green waistcoat, useless; one pair of boots, without soles or heels; a green feather; and a helmet not worth sixpence." A meagre outfit, certainly, to cover the little fever-worn frame; for the mizzling rains and the damp ground and the wretched inaction already spoken of have brought on sickness, and he is now thinner and paler than ever. The service on the staff in Ireland was short. The Commander-in-Chief had that sense of humanity without which a soldier is only a butcher, and, like Moore and Abercromby, he quarrelled with the Irish Executive of the day, whose idea of government was the scaffold and the triangles. It was the period following the wild revolt of Emmett. The hangman was busy at his work. "We passed the gibbet in Thomas Street," wrote the Commander-in-Chief's wife in her diary, "which is now fixed there with a rope suspended, and two sentries to guard it, for so many of the rebels are now executed it is in daily use. What a horrible state for a country to be in!" This was in the year 1803, and in 1804 Charles Napier is back in England again. A great sorrow has fallen upon him. His father has just died. "Sarah, take my watch, I have done with time," Colonel Napier said to the beautiful woman who had loved him so well, handing his watch to her as she stood beside his death-bed. Yet Time had not done with him, and no man who reads of George Napier's sons can ever forget the father to whom they owed so much of their glory.

The short peace is over. War with France has been declared. Pitt is again in Downing Street, busy at fresh coalitions, borrowing his half hundred millions a year and scattering them broadcast over Europe, chafing and raging when he looks at the Horse Guards close by, and longing to be able to infuse something of his own spirit into that establishment, yet all the while obliged to put a good face on it and pretend that he thinks the King's generals are as good as any in Europe. When he gets back to his house at Putney he half forgets his worries, and can even laugh at the feeble tools he has to work with. Here is a little glimpse given us by William Napier in this year, 1804, into Pitt's personal experience of some of the commanding officers who at this time were holding the south coast of England in hourly anticipation of a French descent from Boulogne, where Bonaparte and his Grand Army were encamped almost within sight of the Kentish shore. Pitt has come home to Putney, as usual very fagged and tired after the day's work in Downing Street. He drinks half a dozen glasses of port quickly one after the other, his strength and spirits revive with the stimulant, and then he relates the exciting events of the day. A Cabinet Council is going on. At any moment news may come that the enemy is in Kent or Sussex. Anxiety is strained to fever pitch. Suddenly a dragoon is heard thundering up the narrow street; it is a despatch from the south. The man has ridden in hot haste. The packet is addressed to the Prime Minister. Amid breathless expectation Pitt opens the despatch. A night-cap tumbles out! Is it some stupid hoax? Not at all. One of the ministers has been spending a day or two at the military headquarters on the south coast; he has forgotten his night-cap, and the general, with a keen eye to the importance of ministerial interest, has sent a mounted express bearing the lost head-gear to its owner!

Another evening the Prime Minister tells them that he had that day received a despatch announcing the landing of French troops from two ships at three different parts of the coast! As may be supposed, from these and other instances of military sagacity, the Napier estimate of our generals was at this period not a high one. "It is d—d easy to be a general," we find William writing in 1807; and three years earlier Charles tells us that "most of our generals are more obliged to the Duke of York than to the Deity for their military talents." But perhaps the most absurd instance of the state of military command in England at that time is to be found in a letter written by a general officer very high in command to a notorious lady of the period,[1] in which, describing his inspection of the army cantoned between Dover and Hastings, he tells his correspondent that "from Folkestone he had had a good view of the enemy's works at Boulogne"—an instance of far-sighted reconnaissance not easily to be paralleled in the annals of war. It is really difficult to read with patience in the diaries and letters of the subordinate officers the state of military mismanagement that existed at this time. We have heard a good deal in recent years of the evil done by letting the light of public opinion into military administration; but if men care to know what happened to our army when the Press was gagged, when authority strutted its way from blunder to blunder unchecked by the fear of public censure, they should study the military history of the early years of the century from the rupture of the Peace of Amiens to the campaign of Corunna. Here is a little glimpse of the interior economy of a regiment quartered in the healthiest part of England in the year 1807. Charles Napier is now in the Fiftieth Regiment, quartered at Ashford in Kent. "Our men," he writes, "have got the ophthalmia very badly, and are dying fast also from inflammation of the lungs caused by the coldness of the weather and bad barracks; in some cases typhus supervenes, but is not contagious. There is no raging fever, cold alone is the cause, yet the men die three or four a day. No officer suffers; they are warmer." This was in the month of March. But two months later, in May, the story is not better. "The soldiers have got pneumonia at Hythe," he writes, "and are dying as fast as we folks at Ashford. Only think of a surgeon taking in one day one hundred and sixty ounces of blood, and the man is recovering! They say bleeding to death is the best way of recovering them!" And all this time a very savage and inhuman discipline was going on. Nine hundred lashes was a common punishment for a trifling offence. Both William Napier and Charles Napier have left us many terrible pictures of "the ferocity of a discipline which was a disgrace to civilisation." Writing of the campaign of 1793-94 in Flanders Sir Robert Wilson is still more emphatic. It was a common sight, he tells us, to see a court-martial sitting in the morning the members of which were not yet sober after the debauch of the previous night, but still sentencing unfortunate private soldiers to nine hundred lashes for the crime of drunkenness, the punishment being inflicted summarily in presence of the still inebriated dispensers of justice!

In the autumn of 1805 the most pressing danger of French invasion passed away. Pitt had raised another vast coalition against France. The Austrians and the Russians were again moving towards the Rhine. Then from the cliffs of Boulogne the great captain, now Emperor, turned off to begin that famous march across Europe which in sixty consecutive days carried him to Vienna, taking by the way sixty thousand prisoners, two hundred cannon, ninety standards, great stores of the material of war, and doing this prodigious damage to his enemy with trifling loss to himself, and as a prelude only to the vaster victory he had yet to gain over his combined antagonists on the field of Austerlitz. Still the same dreary round of garrison routine life went on in England. From his monotonous billet in Bognor, Hythe, or Shorncliffe, Napier watched with anxious and yearning eye the great deeds of war which were being enacted at Jena, Auerstadt, and Eylau. It is evident from his journal that at this time he had learned to read with accuracy between the lines of the Government despatches from the seat of war, and the "crushing defeats of Bonaparte" by the Prussian or Russian armies, which so frequently appeared in the *London Gazette*, were read by him with considerable reservation. On February 6th, 1807, we find him discounting the "victory at Pultusk" with these words: "Bonaparte's defeat at Pultusk is dwindling to a kind of drawn battle, which is probably drawing and quartering for the poor Russians."

After the victory of Friedland in June 1807, Napoleon stood at the very summit of his glory. The armies of Austria, Prussia, and Russia had been vanquished in three colossal combats. This Corsican captain had utterly upset all existing theories, contradicted all previous facts, refuted all accepted certainties. He had made a winter campaign in the northern provinces of Prussian and Russian Poland, seven hundred leagues from Paris, and had vanquished his combined enemies at their own doors. It seemed as though destiny had determined to erase for ever from Europe the feudal tradition and the hereditary principle, and to write across the Continent the names of one man and one nation—Napoleon and France. From the raft at Tilsit Bonaparte went back to France to begin these great legislative, industrial, and commercial works which still remain prouder memorials of his greatness than even his most brilliant victories. It was in the midst of these peaceful but ceaseless labours that the little cloud arose beyond the Pyrenean frontier of France which was destined to exert so deep an influence upon his fortunes. Although there existed many and powerful reasons to justify the intervention of France in the affairs of Spain in 1808, it is certain that the course followed by Napoleon on this occasion was neither in keeping with his true interests nor with the policy which had hitherto guided his actions. The state of Spain was notoriously wretched: the treachery of the king and his minister towards Napoleon had been clearly established during the critical period preceding the battle of Jena; but nevertheless, admitting all these facts as politically justifying the French invasion of the Peninsula, there were still stronger and better reasons in favour of non-intervention. Spain was the land of contradictions; the country was the best in Europe for irregular warfare, and the worst for the operations of regular armies. Long before this time it had been well defined as a land where a small army might be defeated, and where a large one would be sure to starve. But beyond all these reasons for non-intervention was the great fact that in invading Spain Napoleon was departing from the rule which hitherto had regulated his action. He was the first to draw the sword. Early in the year 1808 the people of the Peninsula rose in arms against the French. On the field of Baylen a French division was overpowered. The effect of the defeat was electrical; the whole nation was in revolt. Joseph Bonaparte quitted Madrid, and the French withdrew behind the Ebro. The moment was deemed auspicious by the British Government for trying once more the fortunes of a continental war, and in the middle of the year a large English army was despatched to the Peninsula. In the second division of that army Charles Napier sailed for Lisbon to begin his long-wished-for life of active service; he was then twenty-seven years of age. When this second division reached its destination the first phase of the war was over. Vimeira had been fought, the Convention of Cintra signed, and the three generals, Wellesley, Burrard, and Dalrymple, had gone home to appear before a court of inquiry to answer for the abortive result of the campaign. By this strange incident Sir John Moore became Commander-in-Chief of the English forces in Spain, in spite of the elaborate manœuvres of those members of the British Cabinet who had so laboriously planned to keep him out of that position, and in the autumn of the year the march from Lisbon, which was to end at Corunna, began.

In this long and eventful march the three brothers Napier, Charles, George, and William, all young soldiers thirsting for military distinction, came together for the first time since they had quitted the Eagle's Nest at Celbridge. We must glance for a moment at the field of combat which was now opening before these young soldiers. In the month of October, 1808, when Moore began his march from Lisbon, the Spanish armies, some seven in number, formed a great curved line of which the Somo Sierra between Madrid and the Pyrenees was the centre, while the flanks touched the Mediterranean on one side and the Bay of Biscay on the other. Within this curve, with its back to the Pyrenees and its face to the Ebro, lay the French army. Napoleon was still engaged far away in France with his harbours, canals, roads, and codes of law; but his soldiers were already moving from the Rhine to the Pyrenees, and a storm little dreamt of by either the English or the Spaniards was about to burst from the defiles of these snow-capped mountains. The objective of Sir John Moore's march was the north of Spain. So vague was the knowledge possessed by the British Government of the actual condition of affairs in the Peninsula and of the power of the French Emperor that the wildest anticipations of speedy success were indulged in by the English Government at this time, and it was confidently expected that Moore's junction with the Spanish armies would be the prelude to the passage of the Pyrenees by the combined forces and the conquest of France. We have already indicated the position of these Spanish armies in this month of October, 1808. At the close of the month Moore was well on his march into Spain. Napoleon was still in Paris; but all was now ready for the swoop. Early in November he passed the Pyrenees, struck right and left with resistless force upon the Spanish armies on his flanks—first annihilating Blake and Romana at Gamoual and Espinosa, then destroying Palafox and Castanos at Tudela; and finally, breaking with his cavalry the Spanish centre, he forced the gorges of the Somo Sierra, and appeared before the gates of Madrid before the English army had time to concentrate at Salamanca. Never was victory so complete. To fall back upon Lisbon was now the duty and the desire of Sir John Moore, but he was not permitted to follow this course which was so clearly the right one. Yielding to the importunities of Mr. Frere, the English minister to the Junta, Moore abandoned his communications with Lisbon, and directed his march to the north with the intention of attacking the right of the French army now in Leon. It was Christmas when Napoleon heard in Madrid of this unexpected movement of the English army almost across his front. Divining at once the object of the English general, he quitted Madrid, crossed with his guard and a chosen corps the snow-choked passes of the Guadarrama, and, descending into Leon, was in the rear of the English army before Moore had even heard of the movement. It was no wonder that Napoleon should have been almost the bearer of the tidings of his own march; for in ten days, in the depth of winter and in a season of terrific snow and storm, he had marched two hundred miles, through some of the worst mountain roads in Spain. The bird that would forestall the eagle in his flight must be quick of wing. Then began the race from Sahagun, first to Benevente and then to the sea at Corunna. No space now to dwell upon that terrible march—more terrible in its loss of discipline and failure of the subordinate officers to hold their men in command than in stress of fatigue or severity of weather.

What would have been its fate if Napoleon had continued to direct the pursuit can scarcely admit of sober doubt; but other and more pressing needs than the pursuit of the English army had called him away to distant and vaster fields of war.

FOOTNOTE:

[1] Mrs. Mary Anne Clarke.

CHAPTER III CORUNNA

When Sir John Moore, on January 10th, 1809, reached the summit of the last hill that overlooked the city and harbour of Corunna, he beheld a roadstead destitute of shipping. "I have often heard it said that I was unlucky," he remarked to his aide-de-camp, George Napier, as they climbed the land side of this eminence; "if the ships are not in the harbour, I shall believe in my evil fortune." There were no ships in sight, and the heart of the gallant soldier must have known a pang such as can come to few men in life. Yet fate, though seemingly so cruel at this moment, was, as she often is, kind and merciful even when striking hardest. Had the winds blown that would have permitted the fleet to move from Vigo to Corunna, the whole English army would have embarked on January 11th and 12th before Soult had concentrated his pursuing columns; there would have been no battle of Corunna, and the memory of Moore would not have been a deathless pride to his countrymen. When the ships hove in sight on the evening of the 14th the French divisions were lining the heights in front of the British position; and on the morning of January 16th the British army, now reduced to fifteen thousand men, drew up in line of battle on the crest of the sloping ridge which covered Corunna to the south. The sick and wounded had been already embarked, the magazines blown up, the cavalry and artillery horses killed, and nothing remained but to strike with the infantry a last blow for honour. Three weeks earlier, when the first retrograde movement from Sahagun to Benevente had become imperative, Moore issued an order to his army which contained words of very significant import. The disorder of the troops had already commenced, and the officers, some of them of high rank but completely ignorant of the real state of affairs, had begun those murmurs and criticisms to which more than to any other cause the disasters of the retreat were to be traced. After telling his soldiers that they must obey and not expect him to tell them the reason of the orders he gave them, the General went on: "When it is proper to fight a battle he will do it, and he will choose the time and place he thinks most fit; in the meantime, he begs the officers and soldiers of the army to attend diligently, to discharge their parts, and to leave to him and to the general officers the decision of measures which belong to them alone." Now the time and place had come. Nothing but Moore's knowledge of the situation had saved his army from falling at Benevente into the grasp of the giant who had seemingly annihilated time, space, and mountains in order to crush him; but matters were now different. Napoleon was already in Paris, and not more than twenty thousand tired Frenchmen stood over yonder on the parallel heights beyond Elvina, with scant supply of food and ammunition; while he was here at Corunna, with well-stocked magazines, his soldiers recruited by a three days' rest, new muskets in their hands replacing the battered and broken weapons of the retreat, and the *morale* and discipline of his army restored by the magic touch of battle.

The forenoon of the 16th passed without any hostile movement. Both armies faced each other on the opposing ridges—so near, indeed, that the unassisted eye could trace the slightest stir on either side across the intervening valley. Such things are not possible now. The zone of fight has been pushed back by modern weapons to distance that has taken from war all the pomp and pageantry that used to attend rival armies drawn up for battle. The narrow valley that lay between the armies was dotted with villages set amid vineyards. Three of these villages were held by the English pickets, and the right village of the three, Elvina, marked the front of that part of the British line where it curved back towards Corunna, forming a kind of salient to the more extended French line of battle which overlapped our right flank. At this critical point in the English position stood the brigade to which Napier's regiment, the Fiftieth, belonged, the Fourth and the Forty-Second being the other battalions completing this brigade. Opposite, on the French side, Mermet's division was drawn up; but more formidable still were the muzzles of eleven guns—eight and twelve-pounders—which from a commanding height, and only six hundred yards from the village of Elvina, threatened to obliquely rake the English line.

As the morning wore on without hostile movement on the part of the French, Moore, believing that his enemy did not intend to accept the battle he had offered since the preceding day, made preparations to embark his army during the coming night. His reserve, being nearest the roadstead, was to leave the shore as soon as dusk set in, and one by one the brigades opposite the French were to fall back under cover of darkness to the town, and there enter the boats which were to carry them to the ships. These arrangements having been made, the General mounted his charger in Corunna about one o'clock P.M. to visit his army and give the necessary directions for the movement to the shore. He moved slowly out with a heavy heart. Fate seemed steadily set against him. The enemy in front would not attack, and beyond the sea—there, where these vessels were so soon to carry him and his army—he knew but too well that there was another enemy waiting to write him down and vote him down, and to heap sneer and censure upon his actions. All at once there came the sound of a heavy cannon. Another and another shot rolled round the echoing hills. The fine face flushed with the light of hope, spurs were driven deep into the charger's flanks, and, galloping at full speed along the rocky causeway, Moore was soon upon the field—the battle of Corunna had begun.

The right wing of the English army, standing in line on the ridge above the village of Elvina, was exposed to the full force of the eleven-gun battery, whose cannonade had thus opened the battle. Napier's regiment, the Fiftieth, stood just over Elvina, his pickets occupying that village. As each shot gave the enemy a better distance for the succeeding ones, the range was soon found, and the round shot, falling with accuracy upon the line, tore gaps through it and ploughed the surface of the surrounding ground. For a time the men stood silent and motionless under this trying ordeal, but as increasing accuracy caused more frequent casualties in the ranks, a murmur arose from the soldiers, and the cry of "Where is the General?" was audible along the line. Of all the work of war, that of standing steady doing nothing under fire tries the nerves most sorely, and as at this moment in the opening scene at Corunna the forward movement of the French columns became visible, it was no wonder that anxiety for the presence of the chief in whom they so implicitly believed should find vent in words. They had not long to wait the answer to their question. We have seen how the first sound of cannon had roused Moore from his transient gloom, and made him spur forward along the road from Corunna. The picture of his arrival at the scene of action has been given us by Charles Napier, and there are few more striking bits of battle-painting. Napier is standing in front of his line, his pickets are falling back from Elvina before the advancing French skirmishers; behind the enemy's light troops Mermet's heavy column of infantry is coming on rapidly to the attack, their shouts of *En avant!* rising above the crack of musketry or the boom of the battery whose shot is tearing fast through the line.

> Suddenly (says Napier) I heard the gallop of horses, and turning saw Moore. He came at speed, and pulled up so sharp and close to me that he seemed to have alighted from the air, man and horse looking at the approaching foe with an intenseness that seemed to concentrate all feeling in their eyes. The sudden stop of the animal, a cream-coloured one with black tail and mane, had cast the latter streaming forward, its ears were pushed out like horns, while its eyes flashed fire, and it snorted loudly with expanded nostrils, expressing terror, astonishment, and muscular exertion. My first thought was, it will be away like the wind; but then I looked at the rider and the horse was forgotten. Thrown on its haunches, the animal came sliding and dashing the dirt up with its forefeet, thus bending the General forward almost to its neck; but his head was thrown back, and his look more keenly piercing than I ever before saw it. He glanced to the right and left, and then fixed his eyes intently on the enemy's advancing

column, at the same time grasping the reins with both hands, and pressing the horse firmly with his knees; his body seemed thus to deal with the animal, while his mind was intent on the enemy, and his aspect was one of searching intentness beyond the power of words to describe. For awhile he looked, and then galloped to the left without uttering a word.

Shortly after, Moore came back to the Fiftieth again. The fight had thickened, Elvina had been carried by the French column, and the enemy's light troops had begun to ascend the foot of the British position. Napier asks if he may send his grenadier company down the slope? Moore thinks they may fire upon our own pickets; but Napier tells him that the pickets have already fallen back. "Then send out your grenadiers," replies the General, and away he gallops again to another part of the field. Once more he comes back to where Napier is standing. The round shot are falling thickly about, the enemy's attack is now fully developed, and it is evident he means to try his best at this salient of the position to turn the English right and cut the army from its base; but he has not infantry for such a movement. A large proportion of his total force is cavalry, and they are of little use in the enclosures and high fenced lanes that cover the ground. While Moore stands talking this third time to Napier a round shot from the French battery strikes full between the two men. Moore's horse wheels on his haunches, but the rider forces him to front again, while he asks Napier if he has been hit. "No, sir." Then comes a second shot plump into the right of the Forty-Second, which is next in line to the left. A Highland grenadier has had his leg torn off, and in the agony of the wound he cries out. A wave of agitation begins to pass through the men nearest the sufferer; the gap in the ranks is slower to fill up than when men had fallen who were silent. Moore rides to the spot. "This is nothing, my lads," he says; "keep your ranks; take the man to the rear." Then addressing the wounded man, he says: "My good fellow, don't cry out so, we must bear these things quietly." Then he rode to another part of the field; but soon returning again to the ridge above Elvina, he directed the Forty-Second to descend the slope and attack that place. A fierce struggle ensued amid the enclosures and houses of the village. Napier, seeing the Forty-Second pass his flank, ordered his regiment to advance in line upon the village. He made this movement entirely upon his own responsibility; for except when Moore was present the initiative of command appeared to be wholly wanting among the English generals at Corunna. Passing the Forty-Second, Napier carried his regiment through Elvina, until at the side of the village nearest to the enemy his advance was checked by an overwhelming fire. So deadly was the storm of cannon and musketry at this point that both the colours went down almost together, as the ensigns who carried them were shot. Napier's sword-belt was shot off, and the Fiftieth being the advanced regiment in the battle found itself encircled on three sides by a sheet of fire. Looking to his front, Napier saw the heavy battery now close above him. The idea at once occurred to him to assault it; and gathering by great personal exertions about thirty of his men and three or four officers together, he led them straight upon the battery. But his efforts were useless. The companies had become broken and disordered in carrying the village: the Forty-Second had not continued its advance to Elvina; and no supporting corps was sent to strengthen and secure the success which the Fiftieth had achieved. This forlorn hope leading straight upon the battery went down between a fire which smote them almost as much from their friends in rear as from their enemies in front, and by the time the foot of the steep ascent was gained, Charles Napier found himself almost alone before the enemy. The reason why this bold onslaught upon the battery, which was the key of the French position, was thus allowed to run out into a useless sacrifice of life was easily explained later on, although at the moment Napier, knowing nothing of what was happening in his rear, angrily cursed at the supposed hesitation of his men to follow him. To explain the unfortunate result of this attack we must go back to the original position on the ridge. Scarcely had Napier led the Fiftieth upon Elvina than Moore rode up again to the point where he had before stood, and casting his eye upon the tide of battle flowing below him took in at once the situation. Riding forward in the wake of the Fiftieth, he cheered on that regiment to the attack. "Well done, Fiftieth; well done, *my* majors," he cried; for Napier's promotion to field-rank had been due to his influence, and Stanhope the other major was endeared to him by stronger ties. Charles Stanhope was the brother of the woman to whom Moore a few hours later was to send his last message. When thirty years later men criticised with idle censure the life of Lady Hester Stanhope, they forgot how much she had suffered before they had been born. Austerlitz had broken the heart of her illustrious uncle; her lover and her brother slept on the battle-field of Corunna.

The advance of the Fiftieth and Forty-Second from the ridge had left a gap in that part of the line of battle. Turning to one of his staff, Moore directed him to ride back to the reserve and bring up a battalion of Guards to fill the vacant place; then noticing that some companies of the Forty-Second had got into confusion and were falling back, he called out to that regiment to "remember Egypt," and reminded "his brave Highlanders" that they had "still their bayonets left." It was at this moment that a round shot from the battery on the height struck him. The hurtle and crash of the ball made the cream-coloured charger plunge into the air, and the rider fell backward to the ground, but so firm had been his seat that those who were looking on did not believe the shot had struck, so quietly did he seem to fall. This impression was further strengthened when they saw the tall figure half rise from the ground, while his look sought the enemy's ranks with the same calm and intent expression which his face had before worn. But though no sound or sign of suffering seemed to come between the General's mental consciousness and the battle before him, all the worst hurt that shot can do to poor humanity had been done. The left shoulder had been shattered, the arm hung by a shred, and the flesh and muscles of breast and side had been terribly lacerated. When those who were near became aware of the dreadful nature of the wound they tried to disengage the sword from the mangled side. Who can ever forget the dying man's words as he noticed the kindly attempt: "Let it be. I had rather it should leave the field with me." Then he is placed in a blanket and carried to the rear by some Highlanders of the Forty-Second. By this time a couple of surgeons have come up; but he knows the wound is past human cure, and he tells them to go to the soldiers to whom they can still be of use. As they carry him farther back from the fight he makes the bearers often pause and turn him round again to the front, so that he may see for a little longer how nobly his soldiers hold their ground. When they bring him to his quarters his French servant François is overcome with tears at the sight, but Moore says quietly to him, "My friend, this is nothing." And so the day closes, and darkness brings news that the attack of the enemy has failed, and that the ridge from Elvina to the sea is still held by the British. Then, with the honour of his soldiers safe, he turns to his friends. He forgets no one; the interests of aides-de-camp and of the members of his staff are remembered; he sends messages to many friends—one in particular to Lady Hester Stanhope—and once only his voice fails; it is when he mentions the name of his mother. Then, as the shades of rapidly-approaching death gathered closer, it seemed that the images of the cowardly men at home, who, he felt, were certain

Lightly to speak of the spirit that's gone,

And o'er his cold ashes upbraid him,

arose before his fading vision, for with a great effort he appealed from those "posthumous calumniators" to "the people," suddenly exclaiming, "I hope the people of England will be satisfied. I hope my country will do me justice." That dying hope has been realised. Few names stand in purer lustre than that of Sir John Moore. Fortunately immortality is not always measured by success. The chiefs and people of England, who know so little of real war themselves, are perhaps the hardest censors upon military misfortune. Moore's memory was vehemently assailed by the Ministers and Government officials of the day, who tried to screen their own flagrant shortcomings by calumniating the name of the heroic soldier who was no longer there to answer them, and all the paid scribblers and talkers of the time were busy at their truculent work. But justice came at last, earlier and more conspicuously from the enemies who had fought against Moore than from the nation for whose honour and in whose service he had died. Soult and Ney raised a monument to his memory at Corunna almost at the time when Southey, finding out what the world had long known, viz. that although the King might make him a laureate, nature had not made him a poet, began to attempt to write history and to criticise military genius. But a greater soldier than Soult or Ney had still earlier placed the military fame of Moore beyond the reach of little minds. When Napoleon heard of Moore's march from Salamanca to Sahagun, in December, 1808, he exclaimed, "I shall advance against Sir John Moore in person. He is now the only general fit to contend with me." "Where shall we find such a king?" asks William Napier in a letter written from the battle-fields of Portugal two years after Corunna. Fifteen years later the first volume of the *Peninsular War* appeared, and if the spirits of the illustrious dead can read the books that record their actions on earth, that of Moore might well exclaim, "Where has king found such a chronicler?"

We must go back to Charles Napier, fighting fiercely in the enclosures between Elvina and the great battery, and raging because the supports which might have turned his withered effort into success were denied him. We have seen the reason of this denial. The fall of Moore paralysed the thinking power of those who succeeded to the command. Instead of supporting the attack of the Fiftieth, orders were sent to recall that regiment, and Napier and the few men who were still with him were left alone in the extreme front. This withdrawal from Elvina allowed the French light troops to surround Napier's party. Finding himself thus enclosed in a net, he gathered the few survivors around him and made a dash to cut his way through to the English line, but it was too late. He was surrounded and made prisoner. Both sides would appear to have exhausted their ammunition at this point, and the fight was now entirely of cold steel. It is so full of graphic detail, and gives so many glimpses of national characteristics under stress of battle, that it had best be told in Napier's own words.

> I said to the four soldiers [Irish privates of the Fiftieth and Forty-Second] "Follow me and we will cut through them." Then with a shout I rushed forward. The Frenchmen had halted, but now ran on to us, and just as my spring was made the wounded leg failed, and I felt a stab in the back; it gave me no pain, but felt cold, and threw me on my face. Turning to rise, I saw the man who had stabbed me making a second thrust. Whereupon, letting go my sabre, I caught his bayonet by the socket, turned the thrust, and

raising myself by the exertion, grasped his firelock with both hands, thus in mortal struggle regaining my feet. His companions had now come up, and I heard the dying cries of the four men with me, who were all instantly bayoneted. We had been attacked from behind by men not before seen, as we stood with our backs to a doorway, out of which must have rushed several men, for we were all stabbed in an instant, before the two parties coming up the road reached us. They did so, however, just as my struggle with the man who had wounded me was begun. That was a contest for life, and being the strongest I forced him between myself and his comrades, who appeared to be the men whose lives I had saved when they pretended to be dead on our advance through the village. They struck me with their muskets, clubbed and bruised me much, whereupon, seeing no help near, and being overpowered by numbers and in great pain from my wounded leg, I called out *Je me rend*, remembering the expression correctly from an old story of a fat officer whose name being James called out *Jemmy round*. Finding they had no disposition to spare me, I kept hold of the musket, vigorously defending myself with the body of the little Italian who had first wounded me; but I soon grew faint, or rather tired. At that moment a tall dark man came up, seized the end of the musket with his left hand, whirled his brass-hilted sabre round, and struck me a powerful blow on the head, which was bare, for my cocked hat had fallen off. Expecting the blow would finish me, I had stooped my head in hopes it might fall on my back, or at least on the thickest part of the head, and not on the left temple. So far I succeeded, for it fell exactly on the top, cutting me to the bone but not through it. Fire sparkled from my eyes. I fell on my knees, blinded but not quite losing my senses, and holding still on to the musket. Recovering in a moment I saw a florid, handsome young French drummer holding the arm of the dark Italian, who was in the act of repeating the blow. Quarter was then given; but they tore my pantaloons in tearing my watch and purse from my pocket and a little locket of hair which hung round my neck. But while this went on two of them were wounded, and the drummer, Guibert, ordered the dark man who had sabred me to take me to the rear. When we began to move, I resting on him because hardly able to walk, I saw him look back over his shoulder to see if Guibert was gone; and so did I, for his rascally face made me suspect him. Guibert's back was towards us; he was walking off, and the Italian again drew his sword, which he had before sheathed. I called out to the drummer, "This rascal is going to kill me; brave Frenchmen don't kill prisoners." Guibert ran back, swore furiously at the Italian, shoved him away, almost down, and putting his arms round my waist supported me himself. Thus this generous Frenchman saved me twice, for the Italian was bent upon slaying.

Thus was Napier taken prisoner. From this narrative we get many side-lights upon many subjects. Firstly, the composite character of Napoleon's army in Spain, and the fact that the Frank fights with the chivalry of the true soldier; it is the Italian who is all for murder. Secondly, we find all through this narrative of Napier's that our own soldiers were almost wholly Irish. This Fiftieth Regiment which he commands is called the West Kent, but its soldiers are almost to a man Irish.[2] The Forty-Second man who appears on the scene, although nominally a Highlander, is in reality an Irishman. Now, as we proceed further in the narrative, we come to one of the most singular pictures of a Celtic soldier ever put upon paper.

We had not proceeded far up the lane (continues Napier), when we met a soldier of the Fiftieth walking at a rapid pace. He instantly halted, recovered his arms, and cocked his piece, looking fiercely at us to make out how it was. My recollection is that he levelled at Guibert, and that I threw up his musket, calling out, "For God's sake, don't fire. I am a prisoner, badly wounded, and can't help you; surrender."—"For why would I surrender?" he cried aloud, with the deepest of Irish brogues. "Because there are at least twenty men upon you."—"Well, if I must surrender—there," said he, dashing down his firelock across their legs and making them jump, "there's my firelock for yez." Then coming close up he threw his arm round me, and giving Guibert a push that sent him and one or two more reeling against a wall, he shouted out, "Stand back, ye bloody spalpeens, I'll carry him myself; bad luck to the whole of yez." My expectation was to see them fall upon him, but John Hennessey was a strong and fierce man, and he now looked bigger than he was, for he stood upon higher ground. Apparently they thought him an awkward fellow to deal with. He seemed willing to go with me, and they let him have his own way.

They are soon delivered over to a responsible officer. Napier is kindly treated by all the officers he meets; but the exigencies of war call them away, and he remains for two nights and a day exposed to cold and misery on the hill where the English magazine had been exploded a couple of days before the action. On the second day after the battle he is brought into Corunna and made comfortable in Marshal Soult's quarters. Hennessey had disappeared. It was only long months afterwards that Napier knew what had become of this extraordinary soldier; and his ultimate fate and that of the generous drummer Guibert deserve to be recorded.

On the night following the battle Hennessey disappeared. Before going he had unbuckled Napier's silver spurs, whispering at the same time that it was a measure of safety, as "the spalpeens" would be likely to murder the owner for the sake of the metal. Next morning he was marched off to the Pyrenees, but at Pampeluna he got away from his captors and made back across the whole breadth of the Peninsula for Oporto. On the road he sold one of the spurs, which he had managed to conceal all that weary way by hiding them under his arm. When Soult took Oporto three months after Corunna, Hennessey was again taken prisoner; but when the English crossed the Douro he again escaped by rushing at the sentry upon the prison and killing him with his own musket. When the first British battalion entered Oporto he joined them, marched with them to Talavera, and fought in that battle, where a cannon-ball carried off his cap. Hearing that George Napier was with the army, Hennessey found him out and told him the whole story of his brother's capture, and produced the remaining spur, which he still held on to. Then he returned to England to rejoin the Fiftieth—the regiment was at Hastings at the time. Garrison life did not suit Corporal Hennessey—as he had now become—so, remembering that he had a wife and child in Cork, he obtained a furlough to visit them, and walking across England, appeared in his native town in due time. Napier had meanwhile set out again for the Peninsula. On reaching Cork Hennessey heard this, and at once exclaiming, "Is it gone back and the regiment not with him? Thin, be my sowl, I'll niver stop behind, but it's off I'll be too!" he started back without waiting to see wife or child. On his first arrival in England from the Peninsula he walked to York, where Miss Napier was then living. Charles Napier had charged him on the night of Corunna to give the spurs to her if he succeeded in escaping. Hennessey never forgot the injunction; and at York, more than a year after the battle, he delivered the remaining spur to Miss Napier. They had been originally her gift to her brother when he obtained the rank of major before going to Spain in 1808.

Hennessey went back to the Peninsula and began again the old life of reckless daring, mixed with insubordination, drunkenness, and robbery. At last, in one of the battles of the Pyrenees, a cannon-ball carried off his head—a relief alike to his friends and foes, for the former were ever in fear that death at the hands of the provost-marshal would be his fate. The end of the brave Guibert is not less sad. Napoleon, upon hearing of his humane and gallant conduct, bestowed the Cross of the Legion upon him. Some man with better interest disputed the drummer's right to the distinction, and obtained the cherished decoration for himself. Guibert, enraged at his well-earned honour being robbed from him, forgot his higher honour, tried to desert, was taken and shot. What strange episodes of individual heroism dashed with human nature's weakest traits does war hold in its vast tragedy! What extremes of pathos and absurdity jostle each other daily along the road of conflict! In the fight at Elvina Napier's bosom friend and comrade, Charles Stanhope, was shot dead while leading on his men to support his senior officer then under the French guns. The two men thus fighting so valiantly had each a brother on Moore's staff—George Napier and Edward Stanhope. Both these aides-de-camp long searched for their brothers amid the dead and wounded. Stanhope's body alone was found, for Napier's capture was not known for months after the battle, and he was reckoned among the missing dead. The body of Stanhope was brought back to the bivouac and buried there. His surviving brother was passionately attached to him, and when the moment came to fill in the hastily-made grave he leant over it to take a last look at the dead man's face. At that moment a ball from the enemy struck him, but the thick folds of his cloak, which was worn rolled across his chest, stopped the bullet, and prevented Death from joining together in the same grave the brothers he had shortly before separated.

The army of Corunna reached England in a terrible condition. The men had embarked on the night of the 16th in great confusion, portions of regiments and corps getting on board any vessel they could reach in the darkness, without regard to order or number. No account of killed or wounded was ever obtained; but the total loss from the time the army quitted Portugal in October, 1808, until it arrived in England in the end of January, 1809, was not short of twelve thousand men and five thousand horses, and all its material had also been lost. A wild and impossible enterprise, pushed on against the advice of all trained and capable military opinion by the ignorance of the English Cabinet and its representative Mr. Frere. These people spoke of the genius of Napoleon and his generals as a gigantic bubble which had only to be pricked to vanish. The defeat of a brave but indifferent leader like the Duke of Abrantes at Vimieiro, where all the odds of numbers and surroundings were against him, made them believe that they had only to throw another army into the Peninsula and that it would at once combine with the Spaniards and march to Paris. They mistook Junot, in fact, for that extraordinary combination of Jupiter and Mars whom men called Napoleon Bonaparte, and Moore and his gallant troops paid the penalty of the mistake. Nor did the misfortunes of the soldiers end with the campaign. For months after their arrival in England the hospitals were filled with the fever-stricken victims; and many a soldier who had escaped the horrors of the retreat and the battle of Corunna laid his bones in the military graveyards of the south of England. But the authors of the misfortune did not suffer. Secure in a majority returned by a flagrant system of corruption, they laughed at the Opposition; and society, finding a great military scandal soon to divert it, quickly forgot all about the suffering, the misfortunes, and the glory of the campaign of Corunna.

FOOTNOTE:

[2] "The Fiftieth Regiment, although called the West Kent, was chiefly formed of Irishmen."—Napier's *Military Law*.

CHAPTER IV
THE PENINSULA IN 1810-11—BERMUDA—
AMERICA—ROYAL MILITARY COLLEGE

For two months Napier remained a prisoner with the French, and very nobly did his captors treat him, notwithstanding the intense bitterness of feeling caused in France by the way in which prisoners of war were treated in England. Ney, who succeeded Soult when the latter marched from Corunna for Oporto, allowed his captive to live with the French Consul, supplied him liberally with money, and when an English frigate bearing a flag of truce entered Corunna, permitted him to proceed to England on parole not to serve until exchanged. His death had been officially reported, and when he reached England he was to his family and friends as one risen from the grave. A curious figure he must have presented when his brother George and sisters met him at Exeter on the top of the Plymouth coach, still in the old thread-bare red coat that he had worn at Corunna, out at elbows, patched, and covered with the stains of blood and time. On arrival in England he had sent a scrap of paper to his mother with these lines from *Hudibras*:

I have been in battle slain,

And I live to fight again.

What joy to the poor mother, now a widow and with sight failing, to hear her eldest born was not gone from her, but had come back, notwithstanding his fatigues and many wounds, more determined than ever; for he had now seen war, knew the ins and outs of fighting, and he no longer hoped but was absolutely certain that he could command in battle. After Corunna, they tell us, his whole manner changed. The earnest look of his face assumed a more vehement expression. The eagle had in truth tested his wings and felt his beak and talons, and he knew they were more than equal to the fight of life.

In January, 1810, one year after Corunna, Charles Napier rejoined the Fiftieth Regiment, again in the south of England. Meanwhile another expedition had gone to Portugal, and great events had taken place in the Peninsula. Sir Arthur Wellesley, having driven Soult from Oporto, urged by the Ministry at home and by their representatives in the Peninsula to repeat the movement into Spain which had so nearly ended in the destruction of

Sir John Moore's army, advanced along the Tagus, joined Cuesta, fought the French at Talavera de la Reyna, held his position during the battle but fell back from it two days later, leaving his wounded to be captured by the enemy, and narrowly escaping by a forced march Soult's advancing army, retreated back to Portugal with the loss in killed, wounded, prisoners, and by death from disease of fully one-third of his entire army. The British Government, now feeling certain that the last hour of Napoleon had arrived, all at once resorted to the old idea of foreign expeditions; and two of the largest expeditions that had ever left the British Islands had been despatched to the Continent, one to Italy, the other to Holland. In all the long history of abortive military enterprise there is nothing so sad as this Walcheren expedition. It numbered in its naval and military total eighty thousand fighting men. Its fate has been told with vehement truth by Charles Napier's brother. "Delivered over," writes William Napier, "to the leading of a man whose military incapacity has caused the glorious title of Chatham to be scorned, this ill-fated army, with spirit and strength and zeal to have spread the fame of England to the extremities of the earth, perished without a blow in the pestilent marshes of Walcheren." Thus this year 1809, which had opened upon Charles Napier in the gloom of the retreat to Corunna, ran its course of conflict to find him at its close an impatient spectator of these three mighty efforts in Spain, southern Italy, and on the Scheldt, which, though not unattended by brilliant feats of arms in at least one theatre of hostility, had all, so far as their ultimate object was concerned, left matters precisely where they had found them. For it was not at the extremities of his vast empire that the power of Napoleon was to be successfully encountered. When on the first day of the new year he turned back from the distant Galician frontier to take up the burthen of continental war which Austria, subsidised by England, had so suddenly cast upon him, he realised that in the heart of Europe lay the life or death of his power. The march in the summer of 1809 to Vienna is all old history. Despite the duplicity of Austria, which had succeeded in springing upon him a mine while he was yet unconscious of the impending danger, Napoleon's presence on the Danube was sufficient in a few hours to retrieve the errors of his lieutenants, and to neutralise all the advantages which the selection of their time and attack had already given his enemies. In all the brilliant passages of the *History of the Peninsular War* none record great results in fewer or firmer words than this campaign of 1809 on the Danube. "Then indeed," writes the historian, "was seen the supernatural force of Napoleon's genius. In a few hours he changed the aspect of affairs. In a few days, despite their immense number, his enemies, baffled and flying in all directions, proclaimed his mastery in an art which up to that moment was imperfect; for never since troops first trod a field of battle was such a display of military skill made by man."

Wagram was the result of these brilliant combinations. Once again, as at Austerlitz and Friedland, the decisive blow struck in the centre paralysed all minor successes gained at the extremities; and before the year which had opened with such vast preparation and such glowing anticipation closed, the army of Walcheren had perished, that of Italy had retreated to Sicily, and that of the Peninsula, despite its brilliant achievement on the Douro and its valour at Talavera, had fallen back into the pestilent marshes of the Guadiana, where a third of its force was destroyed by fever.

During the winter of 1809-10 great efforts were made to reinforce the army under Wellington, and in May, 1810, Charles Napier found himself once more in the Peninsula. The campaign in north-eastern Portugal had begun. Ney and Massena, advancing from Leon, took Ciudad Rodrigo and forced Wellington back upon middle Portugal. The marches were long and arduous, the fighting frequent and fierce. The famous Light Division, with its still more famous first brigade, covered the retirement. In this brigade the three brothers came again together. In July Crawford fought his ill-judged action on the Coa, and the Napiers were all in the thick of that hard-contested fray. It was Charles who carried the order to his brother George's regiment, the Fifty-Second, to fall back across the bridge when the French cavalry were swarming through the Val de Mula. William Napier's company of the Forty-Third was the last to pass the river, and it was here that he was wounded. This fight at the Coa was the first battle fought by this famous brigade, Moore's chosen corps. Four years earlier he had shaped them into soldier form at Shorncliffe Camp, for his quick perception had early caught the fact that it was only by a most thorough system of field-drill the power of the French arms could be successfully resisted; and truly did William Napier realise on the Coa the debt his brigade owed to Sir John Moore. "The fight on the Coa," he writes, "was a fierce and obstinate combat for existence with the Light Division, and only Moore's regiments could, with so little experience, have extricated themselves from the danger into which they were so recklessly cast, for Crawford's demon of folly was strong that day. Their matchless discipline was their protection; a phantom hero from Corunna saved them!"

In the heat of this action Charles Napier performed a very gallant action which finds only briefest record in his journal, while whole pages are given to noting "for my own teaching" the errors of the general officer commanding the division. Napier had ridden back to the Forty-Third Regiment—still fighting on the enemy's side of the bridge—after delivering an order upon another part of the field. He finds Captain Campbell wounded. He at once gives the wounded man his horse, and then fights on foot with the Forty-Third through the vineyards to the bridge. Still falling back towards Lisbon, Wellington halted at Busaco and gave battle to

Massena. This time only two of the three brothers were in the field, for William was down with the wound received at the Coa. Charles is riding as orderly officer to Lord Wellington. He is in red, the only mounted officer in that colour, as the staff are of course in blue. When Regnier's corps reached the crest of the position a furious fire was opened upon the British line. The staff dismounts. Napier remains on horseback. "If he will not dismount, won't he at least put a cloak over his flaring scarlet uniform?"— "No, he won't. It is the dress of his regiment, the Fiftieth, and he will show it or fall in it." Then a bullet hits him full in the face, passing from the right of his nose to his left ear, and shattering all before it, and he is down at last. They carry him away, but as he passes Wellington he has strength to wave his hat to his chief; and when they lay him in a cell in the convent behind the ridge of Busaco he is more concerned at hearing the voices of officers who are eating in an adjoining room, and who should be on the ridge under fire, than he is with the torment of his own wound. On the morning of the battle he had received a letter from his mother announcing the death of his sister, and now, while lying wounded in the convent, they come to tell him his brother George has been struck down while leading on his men to charge the French assaulting column.

He was carried away over the rough roads of Portugal, and at length reached rest at Lisbon; for the army on the second day following Busaco resumed its retreat, and Massena was again in full pursuit. The confusion was very great, and the wounded had a dreadful time of it. Wellington was laying waste the country as he retreated, and the army was falling back upon the Lines of Torres Vedras amid a scene of destruction almost unparalleled in the horrors of war. Nevertheless neither the severity of his wound nor the exigencies of the retreat prevented Charles Napier from writing to his mother to assure her of his safety, and to make light of his wounds for her sake. There is something inexpressibly touching in the constant solicitude of this danger-loving soldier towards the poor old mother at home. "I am wounded, dear mother," he writes four days after the battle, and while the confusion of the retreat is at its height; "you never saw so ugly a thief as I am, but melancholy subjects must be avoided, the wound is not dangerous." At last he reaches Lisbon and has more time for writing, and the letters become long and constant.

> Never (he writes) had I a petty dispute with you or heard others have one without thanking God for giving me a mother and not a tyrant. Such as your children are, they are your work. The Almighty has taken much from you, but has left much. Would that our profession allowed us to be more with you. Yet even that may happen, for peace, blessed peace, may be given to the world sooner than we

think. It is war now, and you must have fortitude in common with thirty thousand English mothers, whose anxious hearts are fixed on Portugal, and who have not the pride of saying their three sons had been wounded and were all alive! How this would have repaid my father for all anxieties!... The scars on my face will be as good as medals—better, for they were not gained by simply being a lieutenant-colonel and hiding behind a wall.

The winter of 1810-11 passed away, and in the spring of 1811 Massena retreated from Torres Vedras, first to Santerem, and later to the frontiers of Portugal. Hard marching, harder fighting, and hardest living became the order of the day; for middle Portugal had now been made a desert, and provisions of the rudest description were at famine prices. When the spring campaign opened, Charles, though still suffering from his wound, was off to join the army. In a single twenty-four hours he covers ninety miles on horseback on his little Arab horse Blanco, for news of battle is coming back along the line of communications, spurring him on through night and day over the rough roads that lie between the head waters of the Mondego and the Coa. On the morning of March 14th he is close to the front. Suddenly an ambulance-litter borne by soldiers is seen ahead. "Who is it?" he asks. "Captain Napier, Fifty-Second Regiment, arm broken." Another litter follows. "Who is that?" "Captain Napier, Forty-Third, severely wounded." They halt under the shade of a tree. Charles says a word to each, and then mounts his tired horse and presses on to the front. A few weeks later came the action at Fuentes d'Onoro, and all the desultory fighting until Brennier broke out of Almeida, having first blown it up. Amid these scenes of war Charles maintains the same light-hearted gaiety, and his letters and journals are full of details of action mixed with jokes and funny stories; and yet through all this rugged service he is suffering much from the effects of his wound at Busaco; but his sufferings and privations are a constant source of joking with him, and the hardships of the campaign are borne in the same light-hearted spirit. So hard up are they for food that he envies his wounded brothers over at the depôt of Coimbra, who "are living well," he writes, "while we are on biscuits full of maggots—and though not a bad soldier, hang me if I relish maggots; the hard biscuit bothers my wounded jaw when there is not time to soak it." A month after joining the army he thus describes the daily routine of work: "Up at three A.M., marching at four, and halting at seven o'clock at night, when we eat whatever we can get, from shoe-soles to bread and butter." But physical annoyances are not the only ones he suffers from at this time. Ever since Corunna he has had a grievance with the Horse Guards. Neither with the Duke of York nor with his temporary successor, old Sir David Dundas, is he a favourite; and promotion, although given to every other officer in command of a battalion on the day of Corunna, has been persistently denied to him. His letters and journals contain many allusions to this unmerited treatment, and "old Pivot," as Dundas was named in the army, gets small quarter at his hands. In 1811 the Duke of York again became Commander-in-Chief. Napier is delighted, although he sees little reason to hope for better luck. "The Duke of York's advent will do Napiers no good," he writes, "but indeed old Davy going to pot is luck enough for ten years." At last the tide turns; these Napiers, whose names were in every gazette in the list of wounded, could not well be denied the promotion given freely to men who were idling at home in London, and in the middle of 1811 Charles is nominated to the command of the Hundred-and-Second Regiment—a corps then just returned from Botany Bay, where it had been guilty of grave acts of mutiny and insubordination. It was indeed a change for this ardent soldier to quit the stirring scenes of Peninsular strife and take up the thread of military work in an English station, restoring discipline to a regiment demoralised by a long sojourn in a convict settlement at the very end of the globe. At first he hopes that his new corps will be sent to the Peninsula where the storm of war thickens, as once again the great Emperor is engaged with Russia, and all Europe watches with bated breath the gigantic struggle; but he is to see no more of the Peninsula and its war. After a short stay in the island of Guernsey he sails with his regiment to Bermuda in July 1812, turning away from the great field of European conflict and all those stupendous events which marked the campaign of Moscow. His letters at this period are a curious indication of his inexhaustible energy. Despite the contrast between the real warfare he has just quitted and the dull life on this prison rock of Bermuda, he still sets to work to drill his regiment, to improve its discipline, and to check drunkenness among his troops, as energetically as though barrack-square and orderly-room service had always been his aim. He detests the islands and their people; he cannot make friends with the governor, a pompous old fogey, who has the natural dislike which the official owl has ever entertained towards genius in a subordinate; he is still suffering from his fevers and wounds, but all the same he works away at his regiment, sees that the men get all the ration of bread they are entitled to (although it is usual in this island to dock 25 per cent of the flour for some mysterious fund), and drills officers and men into soldiers. In the midst of all this humdrum work comes the news of the battle of Salamanca, to make the contrast of life still more painful. "These glorious deeds in Spain," he writes, "make me turn with disgust to the dullness of drill, and it is hard to rouse myself to work—*yet duty must be done.*" And all through this Bermudian prison period we find the same devotion to his mother shown in a hundred letters—a devotion which even makes that other love of his life, military glory, lose its fascination for him. On New Year's Day, 1813, he thus writes: "A happy New Year to you, most precious mother, and, old as you are, a great many of them. Oh, may I have the delight of being within reach of you next New Year's Day. I would take another shot through the head to be as near you as I was in Lisbon last year. My broken jaw did not give me half the pain the life we lead here does, and being so far from you." When his brother George marries at this time, he writes: "Blessed mother, George's marriage delights me; you may now in time have a dear animal of some kind with you instead of being left in your old age by a pack of vagabond itinerant sons, getting wounded abroad while you are grinding at home. The interest you have had about us has never been of much pleasure, and the little links of a chain to tie you to life may come—your lost great ones can only thus be supplied."

War between the United States and England had now been declared, and Napier quitted Bermuda in May, 1813, with joy to take his part in a desultory campaign on the American coast. This campaign ended in nothing, and it was little wonder it should have proved abortive. It was three parts naval, two parts military; the men were made up of many nations. There were three commanders, and, as Charles Napier remarks in his journal, "It was a Council of War, and what Council of War ever achieved a great exploit?" Several landings were attempted on the American coast; the town of Little Hampton was taken and sacked, and terrible atrocities committed by the foreign scum of which the expedition was largely composed. The regular troops under Napier and the Marines were guiltless of these atrocities—the Marine Artillery being conspicuous by their discipline. "Never in my life," writes Napier, "have I met soldiers like the Marine Artillery; they had it in their power to join in the sack and refused. Should my life extend to antediluvian years, their conduct will never be forgotten by me."

These fruitless operations on the shores of Chesapeake Bay continued for five months. As usual we find Napier ever busy with his note-book setting down his reflections, tracing from the rocks and shoals of the wrecked expedition valuable charts of guidance for his own future. There are bits scattered through these reflections which should be in the text-books of every soldier. Here is one true to the letter to-day as when it was written seventy years ago.

> Our good admirals are such bad generals that there is little hope of doing more than being made prisoners on the best terms. We shall form three plans, or as many as there are admirals, and to these mine will be added. From all—perhaps all bad—a worse will be concocted, and of course will fail. We failed at Craney Island because two admirals and a general commanded; and a republic of commanders means defeat. I have seen enough to refuse a joint

command if it is offered to me; it is certain disgrace and failure from the nature of things; the two services are incompatible. A navy officer steps on shore and his zeal, his courage, and his ignorance of troops make him think you are timid. A general in a blue coat, or an admiral in a red one is mischief. Cockburn thinks himself a Wellington, and Beckwith is sure the navy never produced such an admiral as himself—between them we got beaten at Craney.

When to this divided command it is added that the plan of operations had been in a great measure conceived by the sapient wisdom of Mr. John Wilson Croker, the Secretary of the Admiralty, and embraced a proposal from that authority to send a frigate to act on the Canadian lakes above the Falls of Niagara, any surprise at ultimate failure will be lessened. From the Chesapeake Napier moved in September, 1813, to Halifax, and shortly after he arranged an exchange into his old regiment, the Fiftieth, then engaged in the Pyrenees. He had now been on active service for nearly five years. He had seen war in almost every phase. Though a young man he was an old soldier; several times wounded, once a prisoner, struck at by disease, weakened by the fevers of the Guadiana, he was here in his thirty-second year as keen for active service as when, fifteen years earlier, he had set out from Celbridge to begin a soldier's career. It is curious to note in his writings how little the nature of the man had changed through all this rough lesson of life. The kings of his childhood still wear their crowns; the love of mother and home are still fresh and bright in his heart; his hatred of tyranny, and contempt of fools are as strong as ever; the thirst for military glory is unquenched; but one feeling has steadily grown and increased during all these years of toil and war and travel—it is his admiration for the man he was fighting against. "From first to last," says William Napier, "the great Napoleon was a wonder to him. Early in life, deceived by the systematic vilification of that astounding genius, he felt personal hatred ... but his sagacity soon pierced through prejudice, and the Emperor's capacity created astonishment, which increased when his own experience as a commander and ruler enabled him to estimate the difficulties besetting those stations, and then also he could better appreciate the frantic vituperation of enemies." We find this feeling of admiration increasing with him as time goes on, and through all his writings we see it constantly breaking out. In 1809 we find him entering in his journal a note on the necessity of making war with energy, ending thus: "If war is to be made, make it with energy. Cato the elder said war should nourish war. Cato was a wise and energetic man. Cæsar agreed with him and Cæsar was a cleverer man than Cato. Bonaparte, greater than either, does the same." Napier was no taciturn holder of opinion; on the contrary, he was ever ready to speak the thought that was in his mind, and to back it up too with the sword that was at his side. Holding such opinions at such a time, it is not difficult for us to conjecture what their effect must have been on the circle of his friends and associates, or how powerfully their expression must have fostered or kept alive the prejudices of power and authority against him. That such prejudice existed against him is very clear. For years he seemed to accept it as the inevitable accompaniment of his liberal opinions, his relationship with Mr. Fox, and his thorough independence of character. He seemed ready to win his grade twice over, to pay double rates of blood and toil for the recognition of reward; but as the years go on we find a change coming over him in this respect, and though to the end of his life he never ceases to laugh at the frowns of favour in high place, the laugh gets harder as age increases, and the almost boisterous ridicule of imbecility in power deepens into cynical contempt. Despite all his anxiety to gain once more the field of European warfare, he was doomed to disappointment. When he reached England from Nova Scotia the long war against Napoleon was over, the Emperor was in Elba, the allies were busy at Vienna, and mediocrity was everywhere in the ascendant. In December, 1814, Charles, finding himself on half-pay, entered the Military College at Farnham; not that it had much to teach which he did not already know, for war is the only school in which war can be learned, but his passion for reading could be better indulged at the college than in any other sphere of existence, and as the making of new history seemed stopped to him by the fall of Napoleon, the next best thing was the reading of old history. Here, then, we find him setting to work in 1814 at the study of history, politics, the principles of civil government, questions of political economy, commerce, poor-law, civil engineering, and international law. He seemed to realise that a time was approaching when the minds of Englishmen, so long diverted from their own affairs by the red herring of foreign politics so adroitly drawn across the trail, would again be bent upon reforming the terrible abuses which had grown up in almost every department of the nation, and that the will of the people and not the opinion of a faction would once more be made the helm of the vessel of state. All at once, in the middle of these studies, the news of "the most astounding exploit that ever established one man's mastery over the rest of his species shook the world"—Napoleon had left Elba and was again in France. As a house built of cards goes down before a breath, so the political edifice which Metternich and Castlereagh and their kind were laboriously building at Vienna fell to pieces at the news. The poor parrot who had been placed in the Tuilleries, caged by foreign bayonets, fled as the eagle winged its nearer flight to Notre Dame, and France prepared once more to shed her blood against the men who sought to force upon her a race of monarchs she despised.

CHAPTER V CEPHALONIA

The Hundred Days were over. Napoleon had played his last desperate stake for victory, and had lost. Charles Napier was not at Waterloo. He had quitted the Military College when the campaign opened, but he arrived too late for the great battle. He joined the army before Cambray, and went with it to Paris, but remained there only a few days. His journals and correspondence for this time are not forthcoming, and consequently we are without his own account of a most interesting period; but his brother's reminiscences of the occupation indicate plainly enough that once the fighting was over, regret for the fall of his idol would have made residence in Paris after Waterloo anything but pleasant to him. He went back to the Military College and bit again at his books. By and by he would make cartridges of them to fire into the rascals who are now robbing and trampling on England. Through the five years that follow the fall of Napoleon, he is at a white heat of rage and indignation with the Government. In 1816 he writes to his mother: "There are two millions of people in England and Ireland starving to enable Lord Camden to receive thirty-eight thousand a year, and to expend it on game and other amusements. It is hard, therefore, to say how long poor rascals who think their children's lives of as much consequence as partridges' eggs may choose to be quiet, or how soon, actuated by an *'ignorant impatience of taxation,'* they may proceed to borrow from Lord Camden." And in truth there was sufficient at this time to make his blood boil at what was going on in England. It was the apotheosis of the Tory squire. The game-laws were worthy of the feudal ages; taxation was terrible; the representation of the people in Parliament was a farce. When retrenchment was forced upon the Ministry they began by cutting down the miserable pensions for wounds and service of soldiers, but they kept intact their own gigantic sinecures. "If I have not a right to my pension," writes Napier to his mother in this year 1816, "I have no wish to keep it; the income must be slender that will not enable me to live in content. Nevertheless, this shows what our Ministers are, who begin by retrenching the incomes of those who have nothing else to live on, and who have fought and worked hard for years on almost nothing to gain that provision; retrenching these but refusing to curtail the thousands they enjoy in the shape of sinecures, besides their large salaries and immense private fortunes; and for those profits doing nothing, unless it be telling men with starving children that they are 'ignorantly impatient of taxation' when they demand that their wives and children may not famish." As the year closes we see the hope of better government grow stronger in Napier's letters. "The people are in motion," he says; "reformation advances at the *pas de charge*, and no earthly power can arrest the progress of freedom." "If reform comes," he says, "the glory of England will be brighter than the battles of the last twenty years have made it." Then comes a very remarkable sentence showing how accurately this fighting student had read the lesson of the time. "The freedom of England being rendered complete, Louis the Eighteenth and his brood will be lost, for our example will be followed all over Europe." Only in context of time did this prophecy err. English reform followed instead of preceded the hunting away from France of the Bourbons. France, despite the terrible cloud she lay under in 1816, was still destined to lead the march of modern progress.

During the two years that he remained at Farnham his letters and journals show how earnestly he entered into the political strife. Cobbett and Burdett are his chiefs; emancipation and reform his watchwords; representation of the people, free food, free press, abolition of privilege, his aims. He thinks the redress of grievances must come quickly, and that "a reform will be effected, though to resist it Castlereagh would risk civil war, I believe; but I do not think he has the power." Should it be civil war, however, his mother need not fear, "for with three sons soldiers, one a sailor, and another a lawyer, it will be hard if you don't swim, for these are the finest trades in such cases." Of course, holding such opinions, promotion for Charles Napier was out of the question. In 1819 he addressed the Commander-in-Chief, again soliciting that he might have his commission as lieutenant-colonel antedated to the period of Corunna. He quoted the cases of Sir Hugh Gough and Sir Colin Campbell, both his juniors, who had received this favour. He mentioned his long and arduous services and his many wounds, but all to no effect. Clearly the man who held that rotten boroughs were not the perfection of representative government, that a Roman Catholic ought to be allowed to make a will and have a horse worth more than five pounds, was fit only for foreign service or active warfare, and quite unsuited to hold a military appointment at home. A foreign post was therefore soon found for him. The Ionian Isles seemed a safe place, and accordingly he is gazetted as Inspecting Field Officer of those islands. He sets out in May, 1819, for this new sphere of action, and passing through France, crosses the Alps and journeys down the length of Italy, everywhere watching and noting as he goes.

In July he reaches Corfu. As Inspecting Field Officer he has nothing to do, but the governor, Maitland, quickly finding out that he has no ordinary officer to deal with, sends him on a mission to Ali Pacha at Yannina, who has already sounded the keynote of rebellion against the Porte, so soon to be followed by the general rising of Greece. In reading the notes and reports made by Napier on this mission one is struck by the rapidity with which he grasps the heart of a very complicated question—a question which is still a vital one to Europe. He sees that the keynote of resistance to Russian dominion on the Mediterranean must lie in fostering the rise and growth of a strong Greek kingdom, and he urges this view upon Maitland as early as 1820, summing up his advice in very remarkable words, which later events fully justified. "The Greeks look to England for their emancipation; but if ever England engages in war with Russia to support the Turks, the Greeks will consider her as trying to rivet their chains, and will support the Russians." Again, in 1821, Napier went to Greece and travelled extensively through the country. As he wanders by the battle-fields whose names will never die he is busy fighting them again with modern armies. On the plain of Chæronea he thinks the marsh in front impassable for guns, and sees how Pindus and Parnassus secure a flank; and at Thermopylæ he notes how the sea has receded from the mountain, but thinks three thousand men instead of three hundred might still hold the position against an army. He visits Corinth, Athens, Argos, sees Thebes, Platea, and Delphos, and on March 20th, 1821, reaches the coast at Lepanto. For two months he has been feeding upon the memories of bygone battle and dreaming dreams of fights to come. A few days after he leaves Greece the insurrection breaks out. Then he gets a short leave of absence to England, and returning to Corfu early in 1822 is appointed Military President in Cephalonia—an island where it is hoped that "the impetuosity and violence of Colonel Napier's character and politics" might find room for action without danger to the State. The island of Cephalonia was at this period a terrible puzzle to the orthodox British official. Violence and robbery reigned unchecked; factions, when not preying upon each other, spoiled the neutral husbandman. Everything was neglected. There were no roads through the island, and the steep mountain ranges cut off the inhabitants of one portion from the other. It was an earthly paradise turned by misgovernment into a hell. How Napier took to the work of regenerating this garden of Eden run to weeds can best be told in his own words. "Do not," he writes to his mother, "expect long letters from one who has scarcely time to eat or take exercise. My predecessor is going home, half dead from the labour, but to me it is health, spirit, everything. I live for some use now."

Here then he sets to work in March, 1822, in his kingdom of sixty thousand souls. He sits in court for six hours daily hearing law-cases, for the ordinary courts of justice have long been closed and martial law reigns; he reforms the prisons, he builds quays and a lazaretto, he drains the marshes, and he lays out two great main roads which are to zig-zag up the mountains and bring the ends of his island together. June comes, but he thrives more and more on this variety of labour. "Health besets me," he writes; "up early and writing till eight, then feed and work in office till twelve—sometimes till three o'clock,—swim, dine, and then on horseback visiting the roads. I take no rest myself and give nobody else any; they were all getting too fat." No wonder under such a governor the island begins to bloom. But he is clearing away the weeds too fast, so at least thinks the new Lord High Commissioner and Governor-General of all the Islands, one Adam by name, who grows jealous of this Cephalonian success. He cannot well attack such palpable improvements as drainage of marshes and road-making, but he has seen that Napier wears mustachios, and he will have them off at any rate, so the order comes to shave—"obeyed to a hair" is the response. Whenever dull and pompous authority attacks this keen Damascus-blade bit of humanity called Napier, authority gets a retort that sends it back laughed at, but brooding over some fresh plan of revenge. Adam with dull persistent enmity nursed his dislike for later time. Men like Napier, prodigal of blow in battle, are ever ready to forget the feud when the fight is over, but the ordinary sons of Adam are not thus generously gifted, and this particular Adam had a long memory for revenge.

As the Greek insurrection develops, the Ionian Islands become a centre of interest. Napier, whose recent travels had made him acquainted with both the people and the theatre of operations, keenly watched the struggle. In August, 1823, Lord Byron arrived at the island on his way to Greece. The intercourse between him and Napier became very intimate. At this period the great poet was almost as unpopular with his countrymen as Napier was with their rulers. Byron's quick wit was not slow to see a leader of men in the Resident. "He is our man," he writes to the Greek Committee in London; "he is our man to lead a regular force or to organise a national one for the Greeks; ask the army, ask anybody; in short, a braver or a better man could not easily be found." Napier was at this time very anxious to get command of a legion to aid the Greeks, but he had been told that if he accepted this position he would probably forfeit his commission in the army, and it was hoped that through the action of the Greek Committee in London his retention in the service might be found compatible with command in Greece. This hope was not to be realised. Napier went to London early in 1824 and had many interviews with the Greek Committee collectively and individually, nor was he much impressed by their wisdom. One member asks him to "make out a list of a proper battering-train to be sent out to reduce Patras." He endorses the request thus: "Square the list of guns and stores needed for a siege with my opinion of spending money so foolishly; men are prone to buy fiddles before they know music." Now all at once he has to answer a serious charge made in high quarters. Mr. Canning, the Prime Minister, has been listening to the stories of German adventurers from the Levant—he has heard that Napier had used his official position in Cephalonia to negotiate with the Greek chiefs. The story was absolutely false, and in straightforward and manly words he told the

Prime Minister that it was so. Indeed one can read between the lines of this reply that he was not sorry to have an opportunity of letting Mr. Canning see his sentiments. "For my part," he writes to Lord Bathurst, "I scorn to deprecate the wrath of any man who suspects my integrity. If, however, your lordship's colleagues either doubt my conduct, or wish for my place to give to a better man, in God's name let them use their acknowledged power to employ men they think best calculated for the King's service." These were strong and daring words to come from a lieutenant-colonel now in his forty-second year, and with nothing but his commission to give him bread, to a Cabinet Minister—the eye of the head of the Government; and what a glimpse they give us of the foundation upon which all this energy and resource and genius for action rested.

In the winter of 1825 he returns again to Cephalonia, this time travelling by Inspruck and the Tyrol to Venice. Blood will tell; he cannot make friends with the Germans. "As to the people of every part of Germany," he writes, "honour to Cæsar for killing so many of them; stupid, slow, hard animals, they have not even so much tact as to cheat well. We always detected their awkward attempts. Out of these regions we descended into Italy, where we found civilised beings, warm weather, and the human face instead of the German visage." This is of course three parts chaff, but it serves to show how the nature of the man blows. And how could it blow otherwise? A soldier who had in his veins the blood of the victor of Ivry, of Mary Stuart, of Scottish chief and Norman noble, and whose whole nature had imbibed in Ireland, in childhood, boyhood, and youth, that "Celtic spell" to whose potent influence our most unemotional historian has borne witness, could no more make friends of the Teutonic type of humanity than an Arab horse in the deserts of the Nile could gambol with a rhinoceros lying on a mud-bank in mid river.

He reaches Corfu in February, after a terrible passage of twenty days from Venice, and here there occurs an entry in the journal which is of interest: "*March 24th.*—Sir Hudson Lowe's colonel, Gorrequer, is here. He called on me, but got not his visit returned. It is not my intent to consort with gaolers, though I have brought out the model of a gaol." Then he goes on to his island kingdom and sets to work at his roads, harbours, and buildings. He is delighted to get back to his Greeks again, and they are equally glad to have their king once more among them. "Now," he writes on arrival, "I am once more amongst my merry Greeks, who are worth all other nations put together. I like to see, to hear them. I like their fun, their good humour, their Paddy ways, for they are very like Irishmen." His intense love of animals is constantly coming out in letter and diary. Blanco, the charger of Peninsula days, he will never abandon. He has brought this old friend out from England, despite his years, paying high for the passage.

"My bill for him and baggage is *only* one hundred pounds. How *honest* John Bull in the city touches one's pocket. Thirty of this is for Blanco, twenty for King, seven for insurance, the rest is cheat and devilment. However, anything is better than cutting Blanco's throat after sixteen years' comradeship. I may go to perdition, but not for Blanco anyways. My poor, good old beast!" Again, as he draws near Cephalonia, he pictures to himself his first visit to his two famous roads, and wishes that, in case of death, he may be buried in the old chapel on the summit of St. Liberale's Mountain, so as to "lie on the top of the road. Many a poor mule's soul will say a good word for me at the last day, when they remember the old road."

Meanwhile the Greek insurrection had run its course of blood and devastation, and as yet out of its four years' chaos of desolation victory had not dawned upon either combatants. Ibrahim, the son of Mehemet Ali, had now carried an army of Egyptian and Nubian soldiers into the Morea, and men, women, and children were being slaughtered by this clever but cruel master of war. Till this time Napier had longed to throw his sword into the scale with the struggling Greeks, but his desire was tempered with a just determination that no premature or foolhardy action should give his enemies the opportunity he knew so well they longed for. He feared to find himself suddenly struck out of the army list, and his service of thirty years with all its toils and wounds thrown away. "When I saw Greece about to rise in strength and glory my resolve was to join her," he says, "if it could be done with advantage to her just cause and honour to myself. The talent of the people, and their warlike qualities, excited my admiration, for a Greek seems a born soldier, and has no thought but war. Their vanity and love of glory equal those feelings with the French, but the Greeks are more like the Irish than any other people; so like even to the oppression they suffer that, as I could not do good to Ireland, the next pleasure was to serve men groaning under similar tyranny."

In the autumn of 1825 the negotiations between him and the Greeks, which had previously fallen through owing to difficulties about his commission in the British army, were again resumed, and matters were all but concluded when a proclamation forbidding officers to serve the Greek cause was published in England. Still Napier was prepared to sever his connection with the army and throw in his lot with the Greeks, provided certain guarantees were given for the equipment and payment of a small regular force, and for the value of his own commission which would be sacrificed by the step. The Greeks in Greece were ready to assent to these propositions, and to any others which Napier might desire to stipulate, so anxious were they now in this dark hour of their fortune to secure his service as Commander-in-Chief; but the bond-holders in London, these curses of all good causes, had their own views as to what should be done, and they were more desirous of spending their money in sending out a useless fleet than in equipping the nucleus of a regular force, which under such a leader as Napier would have been of incalculable benefit to Greece. Thus the whole project fell to the ground, and Napier had to remain in Cephalonia for four years more, and to content himself with his roads and bridges, his purer administration of justice, his efforts to improve the lot of the husbandman, to lessen the unjust privileges of the nobles, to increase the produce of the island, and, harder than any of these things, to battle against ignorance in high places, against the sting of censure from stupidity and intolerance combined in command.[3] Yet in spite of factious opposition and ignorant enmity it is probable that the nine years which Napier spent in the Ionian Isles were the happiest of his life. Who can ever measure the enjoyment of these rides over the mountains and through the valleys of that beautiful island? For, with all the practical energy that marked his character, there was a deep poetic instinct in him that made him keenly sensible of the beauty of nature; while his love of reading, continued since boyhood, had stored his retentive memory with the historic traditions of the past. In a memoir on the Roads of Cephalonia, which he published in 1825, there is a description of the valley of Heraclia, lying on the eastern side of the island, which shows how thoroughly he appreciated beauty of scenery, and how well attuned was his mental ear to catch the music of those wondrous memories which float for ever around the isles and shores and seas of Greece.

But if Cephalonia held for Charles Napier some of the pleasantest memories of life, so did his period of residence in the island mark his final separation from many loved companions of youth. In 1826 his mother died, and the long and most affectionate correspondence which had lasted from the early Celbridge days came to an end. Never indeed was her image to fade from his memory. To the last it was to remain with him, undimmed by distance or by time, coming to him in weary hours of trouble and disappointment, of glory and success; and as at his side in battle he always wore his father's sword, so in his heart he carried the memory of his mother, whose "beauteous face seemed to smile upon me," he tells us, in the most anxious moments of his Scindian warfare.

In 1830 Napier's Ionian service came to an end. He was recalled. It was the old story. Multiplied mediocrity had beaten individual genius. It is not only inevitable, it is even right that it should be so; for by such heating and blowing in the forge of life is the real steel fashioned which has flash and smite in it sufficient to reach us even through the tomb.

FOOTNOTE:

[3] The gratitude of men for toil and service given to them is not so fleeting as people suppose. "They still speak of Napier in Cephalonia as of a god," said a Greek lady to the writer in this year, 1890.

———————————————

CHAPTER VI OUT OF HARNESS

Charles Napier in 1830 was to all human eyes a ruined man. He was close upon the fiftieth year of his age. He was miserably poor; he had a sick wife and two young children to maintain. "Worse than all," he writes, "I have no home, and my purse is nearly empty; verily all this furnishes food for thought." And bitter food it must have been. He was out of employment and under a cloud, for authority, often ready to justify its own injustice, was eager to use its powerful batteries of unofficial condemnation, to hint its doubts and hesitate its dislikes, and find reason for former neglect in this new proof of "temper neutralising brilliant qualities," or of "insubordination rendering promotion impossible." No employment, no home, no money, life's prime gone; toil, service, wounds, disease, all fruitless; and worse than all to such a nature, the tactless sympathy of the ordinary friend, and the scarce-veiled joy of the ordinary acquaintance—for the military profession is perhaps of necessity the one in which the weed of jealousy grows quickest, and nowhere else does the "down" of one man mean so thoroughly the "up" of another. When the shell takes the head off "poor Brown" it does not carry away his shoes, and Jones is somewhere near to step into them.

Failure at fifty is terrible. The sand in the hour-glass of life is crumbling very fast away; the old friends of childhood are gone; a younger generation press us from behind; the next turn of the road may bring us in sight of the end. We have seen in the preceding chapters the extraordinary energy of Charles Napier in action. We shall now follow his life for ten years through absolute non-employment, and our admiration will grow when we find him still bearing himself bravely in the night of neglect, still studying the great problems of life, still keeping open heart to all generous sympathies, and never permitting the "slings and arrows of outrageous fortune" to drive him into the regions of apathy, callousness, or despair.

In the year 1830 England was in a strange state. The reform which sanguine men had looked for as close at hand fifteen years earlier had not yet come, but many things had come that had not been expected. France had shaken off the Bourbons; Belgium had shaken off the Dutch; the people had in fact righted themselves. The example was contagious. Throughout the length and breadth of England there arose an ominous murmur of discontent. It was clear that the limit of patience was being quickly reached, and if Parliament would not reform itself it ran a fair chance of being reformed in spite of itself. The accession of William the Fourth, the manifestation of the supremacy of popular will on the Continent, and the increasing pressure given by depression in manufacture and agriculture, all joined to produce a general conviction that the moment had arrived when reform could no longer be delayed. What then must have been the dismay and indignation of all men who were not blinded by faction to the true interests of England when in November, 1830, Wellington delivered in the House of Lords his famous anti-reform speech, telling the astonished country that the existing representative system possessed the full and entire confidence of the country, that any improvement on it was impossible, and that "so long as he held any station in the Government of the country he should always feel it his duty to resist any measure of parliamentary reform." This speech was read as a declaration of war. A fortnight after its delivery the Duke resigned office, the Whigs came in, but they sought rather to fence with the question than to solve it. The excitement became more intense, the country was literally as well as figuratively in a blaze. In the north of England incendiary fires burned continuously. In March the first Reform Bill was brought in by the Whigs; incomplete and emasculated though it was, to suit the tastes of opponents, it was still thrown out. Then Brougham, seeing that the hour had come for reform or revolution, stepped to the front, forced dissolution upon the reluctant King, and the great election of 1831 followed. The new House of Commons passed the Bill; the Lords threw it out. Popular rage rose higher than ever. There is one way to save the State. Let the King create new peers, and out-vote this obstinate faction in the Lords which is bent on resisting the will of the people. The King would not take this step, and the tide rose still higher. Bristol was burnt. The funds were down to seventy-nine. The windows of Apsley House were broken. The Duke of Newcastle's castle at Nottingham was destroyed by the mob. Indignation meetings were everywhere convened to protest against the action of the Lords. An enormous meeting of one hundred and fifty thousand persons assembled in Birmingham, and unanimously resolved not to pay taxes until the Bill was passed. The winter of 1831-32 was spent in fruitless debates. "There is no hope but in violence; no chance of escaping a revolution," writes William Napier. In May, 1832, Lord Grey resigned because the King would not create new peers. Wellington was sent for by the King; for a fortnight he endeavoured to frame an anti-reform ministry, and then it was that popular indignation broke through all bounds and carried everything before it. The King had to come from Windsor to London, and from Hounslow to Buckingham Palace one long shout of discontent greeted the royal carriage. "No taxes until Reform"; "Go for gold and stop the Duke," were the cries that met Wellington when he drove to meet His Majesty at the Palace. A few days later he was mobbed and pelted with all kinds of missiles as he rode through the city. To make the insult more ominous it was the anniversary of Waterloo. Then the King gave way. Brougham and Grey came back to office, the Lords surrendered, and the Reform Bill became law.

It was into this seething state of politics that Charles Napier came back from the Ionian Isles. During the three years following his retirement from active employment, the pressure from straitened means, and the sense of injustice under which he laboured, kept him much to himself. The terrible epidemic of cholera which swept England in 1832 very nearly made him one of its victims. Scarcely had he recovered from this fell disease than he was struck down by a terrible blow. In the summer of 1833 his wife died. Then at last the great heart of the man seemed to break. A leaf from his written thoughts at this time attests the agony he endured. "O God, merciful, inscrutable Being," he writes, "give me power to bear this Thy behest! Hitherto I had life and light, but now all is a dream, and I am in darkness, the darkness of death, the loneliness of the desert. I see life and movement and affection around me, but I am as marble. O God, defend me, for the spirit of evil has struck a terrible blow. I too, can die; but thus my own deed may give the dreadful spirit power over me, and I may in my haste to join my adored Elizabeth divide myself for ever from her. My head seems to burst. Oh, mercy, mercy! for this seems past endurance." What depths of agony these heroic natures know, as profound as the heights they climb to are immense! He arose from this sorrow chastened, but at the same time steeled to greater suffering. He hears that his enemies in London and Corfu are about to attack him in the Reviews. "I will assail in turn," he writes. "I am so cool, so out of the power of being ruffled by danger, that my fighting will be hard. The fear of being taken from my wife to a gaol made me somewhat fearful, when I wrote before, now I defy prosecution and every other kind of contest." In the end of 1833 he settled at Caen in Normandy. His life now was very dreary, and his letters show how small are the sorrows of disappointed ambition compared with the blows which death deals to all. "Formerly," he writes, "when looking down from Portsdown Hill on Broomfield, which contained my wife and children, how great was my gratitude to God! My heart was on its knees if my body was not." Six months after his loss he writes: "I am well aware my fate might be much worse, but all my energy cannot destroy memory. This morning my eyes fell on the account of Napoleon bursting into tears when meeting the doctor who had attended Josephine at her death—what he felt at that moment I feel hourly, yet I am cheerful with others. My grief breaks out when alone—at no other time do I let it have its way; but when tears are too much checked, comes a terrible feel [sic] on the top of the head, which though not real pain distracts me, and my lowness then seems past endurance." Then he turns to the education of his two daughters, and lays down rules for their training, the foundation of all to be "religion, for to this I trust for steadiness." So the time passes. He remained in France for three years, and early in 1837 came back to England, taking up his residence in Bath. During these three years of absence he had been busy with his pen. His book on *Colonisation* had been followed by one on *Military Law*, a work the name of which very inadequately describes its nature, nor had he been left altogether outside the pale of official recognition, for in 1835 efforts were made to induce him to accept an appointment in Australia. These efforts were unsuccessful, and perhaps it was best that they should have failed, for, as in his book on *Colonisation* he had openly avowed his intention of guarding the rights of the aborigines, "and of seeing that the usual Anglo-Saxon method of planting civilisation by robbery, oppression, murder, and extermination of natives should not take place under his government," it is more than doubtful whether even his success in a Colonial Government could have been possible. It is singular to note in his views of colonisation how early he understood that Chinese labour could be made available to rough-hew a new country into shape. As to his general idea of government, it is summed up in a dozen words—words which should be nailed over the desk of every Government official from the Prime Minister to the humblest tide-waiter. "As to government, all discontent springs from unjust treatment. Idiots talk of agitators; there is but one in existence, and that is *injustice*. The cure for discontent is to find out where the shoe pinches and ease it. If you hang an agitator and leave the injustice, instead of punishing a villain, you murder a patriot."

But this work was far more than a treatise upon Colonisation. A large portion of it was devoted to the exposure of the fatal effects inevitable from the system of large farm-cultivation then, and for so many years after, in wildest swing. Living in France at the time, he was able to compare the general level of comfort enjoyed there by the small proprietor with the misery of the labouring class in England. The boasted "wealth of England," he scornfully remarks, "is to her vast poor and pauper classes as the potato and 'pint' of the Irish labourer; the Irish may point his potato towards the wretched rasher suspended above the table, the English poor may speak with bated breath of the wealth of their country, but they are not to get the smallest taste of it." Clearly he predicts the day when the landed interest shall suffer for their accumulated sins, and he addresses them in anticipatory language such as Hannibal spoke in scorn to the Carthaginian Senate when they wept over the disasters of Carthage. "Ye weep for the loss of your money, not for the loss of your people. I laugh at your anguish, and my scorn for you is sorrow for Carthage." A book full of sense, of long and widely gathered experience, of keen and trenchant reflection, all aflame against stupidity, wrongdoing, and official blundering; all abounding with sympathy for the weak, for the oppressed, for the suffering.

Shortly after his return to England his other book on *Military Law* was published. As we have already said, the title was misleading. The work treated on many subjects besides Military Law, and touched on a thousand points of military interest. It is in fact an elaborate treatise upon soldiers, their peculiarities, their virtues, and their shortcomings. He recalls with pride the fact that it was not at the door of the regular soldiers the atrocities of 1798 in Ireland could be laid, and remembers how when Hamilton Rowan's house was searched by the military, a single silver spoon that was taken was restored to its owner, although, adds Napier at the time, "I saw the Castle of Dublin filled with the rich and powerful, many among them daily robbing the silver spoons of the public." But in this book, as in all his writing, there is one subject upon which he is never tired. It is the man in the ranks. How intimately he knew that man, how truly he loved him, all these multiplied pages of journals, letters, and books tell. He has not the gift of that sublime and eloquent language in which his brother has made the deeds of the British soldier in the Peninsular War immortal—that English classic which, like a stately temple of old, so grand amid the puny efforts of later architecture, stands out amid modern word-building in a magnificence of diction that becomes more solemn and stately with the growth of time; but if this rare gift is wanting in Charles Napier, every pulse of his own soldier nature beats for the man in the ranks. He has seen him at all times and in all places. He knows his weakness and his heroism; he is never tired of labouring for his improvement or his benefit. The word "soldier" in his eyes obliterates national boundaries and abolishes the distinctions of creed, colour, or country. He can love and admire the soldiers who are fighting against him, provided only that they fight bravely. The French drummer who saved his life at Corunna is never forgotten. "Have I a right to supporters?" he asks, when he hears he has been made a Knight of the Bath. "If so, one shall be a French drummer for poor Guibert's sake." The chief purpose he had in view when writing on Military Law was the abolition of flogging, at least in peace time, in the army. "It is odious and unnecessary in peace," he writes. "Our father was always against it, and he was right. The feeling of the country is now too strong to bear it longer, and the Horse Guards may as well give way at once as be forced to do so by Parliament later on." This was in 1837, but more than forty years had to pass before the "cat" was done to death.

When the general election took place in 1837 Napier was in Bath, where politics were running very high. Roebuck contested the seat in the Radical interest and was beaten. Charles Napier supported him with might and main, and his comments on the election are curious. "The Tories, especially the women, are making a run against all the Radical shops. Can we let a poor devil be ruined by the Tories because he honestly resisted intimidations and bribery? Nothing can exceed the fury of the old Tory ladies." Evidently many things in this world are older than they seem to us to-day.

Napier had reached his fifty-sixth year; for eight years he had been unemployed. He was now a major-general, but his half-pay was wretchedly inadequate to his necessities, and he felt that the shadow of age could not be much longer delayed. Poverty, neglect, old age, obscurity—these were the requitals of a life as arduous, as brave, as honourable, and as devoted to duty as any recorded in our military annals. Fired by the news that he was again to be passed over for some appointment, he made in this year, 1838, a last appeal for justice. In this letter he reviews his long service, beginning at Corunna thirty years earlier. He shows how junior officers who had served under his orders had received rewards and promotion, and how favours denied to him as "being impossible" had been given to others whose record of battle and wound had not been equal to his own. In the end of the letter the fear that is in his heart comes out. He hopes that "consideration may be shown to his long services—services which at fifty-six years of age cannot be much longer available." Still no work for this tireless worker. Then he goes back to his books, writes a romance called *Harold*, edits De Vigny's *Lights and Shades of Military Life*, and turning his attention again to Ireland, publishes an essay addressed to Irish absentees on the state of Ireland. But now the long night was wearing out. In March, 1839, he received in Ireland, where he has been living for six months, a summons from Lord John Russell. He proceeds at once to London, is offered and accepts the command of the northern district, where the working classes, justly enraged at having been used by the Whigs to wring reform from their enemies, and then flung aside and denied all representative power, were now combining in dangerous numbers to force from the men they had put in office the several reforms of the Constitution which were grouped under the title of Charter. Taking from the example of the Whigs the threat of physical force which that party had not scrupled to use in their struggle for reform, the Chartists openly avowed their intention of redressing their wrongs by arms. In offering the command of the north of England to Napier the Government showed signal judgment, for on all the important points of the Charter—vote by ballot, manhood suffrage, and short parliaments—he was himself a Chartist; but he well knew that of all evils that can visit man that of civil war is the very worst, and while on the one hand he would tell the governing powers that the tide of true popular right can only be finally regulated by the floodgates of concession timely opened, he would equally let destructive demagogues know that if physical force was to be invoked he, as a soldier, was its master.

CHAPTER VII
COMMAND OF THE NORTHERN DISTRICT

In the spring of 1839 Napier assumed the command of the north of England. The first entry in his journal is significant. "Here I am," he writes on April 4th in Nottingham, "like a bull turned out for a fight after being kept in a dark stall." He had been in this dark stall for more than nine years. He had just arrived from London, where he had had many interviews with Lord John Russell and other governing authorities. That these glimpses of the source and centre of power had not dazzled his mind out of its previous opinions another extract from the journal will show. "Lord John Russell and the Tories are far more to blame than O'Connor in my opinion. The Whigs and the Tories are the real authors of these troubles, with their national debt, corn-laws, and new poor-law."

The condition of England at this time was indeed precarious, yet it was inevitable. The remedy of reform, delayed until the last moment of an obstinate opposition, had excited hopes in the minds of the masses that could not be realised. "The poor you will have always with you." As well might the victim of hopeless disease expect to spring from the bed of sickness in perfect health and vigour after the first spoonful of his black draught as the deep-seated poverty of England look for cure in the black letter of the most radical statute; but there is the difference between making the best of the bad bargain of life and making the worst of it, and that is exactly the difference between the men who object to all change and those who hold that change must ever be the vital principle of progression.

But although the operation of laws can only be gradual to cure, however rapid they may be to cause, the great mass of the people of England looked to immediate relief from their sufferings as the certain result of the popular triumph of reform. They were doomed to disappointment on the very threshold of victory. During the last three years of the protracted struggle the Whigs had invoked the physical aid of the people, and there can now be little doubt that it was that physical aid which had finally decided the battle. When Birmingham threatened to march on London, and when enormous masses of people in the large cities of the kingdom pledged themselves not to pay taxes until the Reform Bill was made law, privilege ceased its opposition. But the people had fought for themselves as well as for the Whigs, and when the victory was gained they found the Whigs alone had got the spoils. The people were as much in the cold as ever. The three great anchors of a pure and true representative system of government—the ballot, manhood suffrage, and short parliaments—were notoriously absent from the new scheme. It was only to be a change of masters, and a change that by no means promised well, for the old Tory landholder with all his faults and his prejudices was generally a gentleman, always an Englishman, and often a humane man; but this new mill-lord was often a plutocrat, always a shrewd man of business, and generally one who reckoned his operatives as mill-hands, and never troubled himself about their heads or their hearts. Thus, instead of a sudden realisation of benefit the people found themselves worse off than ever, lower wages, new and oppressive poor-laws, no voice in the law-making, and quite at the mercy, wherever they possessed the limited franchise, of the will of their masters. Little was it to be wondered at, therefore, that in the seven years following reform they should have grown more and more discontented, and that, borrowing from their old Whig leaders the lesson of force so successfully set by those chiefs, they should have everywhere formed themselves into an association prepared to pass the bounds of peaceful agitation in support of their demand for manhood suffrage, the ballot, and short parliaments. All these principles of Chartism Charles Napier well knew long before he accepted the northern command, but of the actual starvation and abject misery of the lower orders in the great manufacturing towns he knew little; and side by side with his military movements and plans in case of attack we find him from the first equally busy in the study of the state of the people, and equally urgent in his representations to the Government, that while *he* would answer for the order and peace of the moment, *they* must initiate and carry out the legislation which would permanently relieve, if it could not cure, this deep distress and widespread suffering.

It is wonderful to mark in his letters, reports, and journals how quickly he has mastered the complicated situation which surrounds him. Three weeks after he has taken command he has the military position secured. He will have three distinct groups of garrisons, with three points of concentration, and plans for separate or for united action. He has all the local magistrates against him, because they alone think of their individual towns, villages, or private houses, and they want troops scattered broadcast over the country. The Bradford Justice of the Peace would willingly see Manchester, Leeds, and Newcastle given to the flames provided his own city had a soldier billeted in every attic; then a great local potentate would suddenly rush off to London and threaten the Home Office with terrible dangers if his particular park had not the three arms surrounding it. Notwithstanding all difficulties Napier works away, gets the troops into strategical positions, and, though he hates the work, throws all his energies into it. Here we have his plans and his opinions four weeks after he has taken command.

> My men should be in three masses, one around Manchester, one around Newcastle to watch the colliers,

one around Leeds and Hull to watch the other two; but such an arrangement of my force can only be effected in time. It would take a month to make the Secretary of State understand it, and then he would have a host of magistrates on his back. He behaves, however, very well, and stands by me against the magistrates, so that I have my own way in some degree. Were it allowed me in all things the country would soon be quieted. Poor fellows! they only want fair play and they would then be quiet enough, but they are harassed by taxes until they can bear it no longer. We could manage a large force of Chartists; but I trust in God nothing so horrible will happen. Would that I had gone to Australia, and thus been saved this work, produced by Tory injustice and Whig imbecility! The doctrine of slowly reforming while men are famishing is of all silly things the most silly—starving men cannot wait; and that the people of England have been and are ill-treated and ill-governed is my fixed opinion. The worship of mammon renders the minds of men base, their bodies feeble, and their morals bad. Manufactures debase man, woman, and child.

All through the summer of 1839 this work goes on. On May 25th a great meeting took place on Kersall Moor near Manchester. It passed over quietly. Napier had concentrated two thousand men and four guns in the vicinity, and he had further taken the original precaution of getting an introduction to a meeting of Chartist leaders, and telling them plainly that if they meant only to lay their grievances before Parliament they would have no opposition from him, and that neither soldier nor policeman would be allowed to disturb them, but that if there was the least disturbance of the peace he would use the force he had to quell it. Another step he took too in this same direction of prevention which should not be lost sight of. He had heard that the Chartists were very confident that their possession of five or six brass cannon was of immense importance to them, and that when the day of action would arrive these guns would give them victory. He at once secretly invites a leading Chartist chief to visit with him the artillery-barrack while the gunners are at work. The battery is drawn up, the command is given to dismount the guns, remount them and come into action. It is done in the usual brilliant and rapid manner, and the Chartist chief goes away from the parade not quite so confident that the five old brass carronades which are hidden away under some backyard rubbish will be equal to meet in action these perfectly served guns.

I have read many things in the life of this soldier, but nothing that does greater honour to him than this desire to use every means in his power to prevent the effusion of civil blood. There is in almost every military mind a pride of arms that tends to prevent a soldier taking any step with his enemies which might even remotely seem to be an avoidance of strife; but in this instance, when civil war is trembling in the balance, when the magistrates and many of the Government officials are calling out for vigorous measures, when Whigs and Tories are jointly agreed that stern repression is to be the rule of politics, we find the real soldier anxious only to avoid spilling the blood of his countrymen, ready to forget his own pride of arms, and to show the leaders of this multitude how useless must be their attempt to right their wrongs by force of arms.

In all this anxious time we find the mind of the man as keen to catch absurdities and note defects of system, military or civil, as it was in the past. Here is a bit of criticism, good to-day as when it was written fifty years ago. "I cannot conceive," he writes to an artillery officer, "how my account of barrack accommodation differs from yours. But this and other difficulties and irregularities proceed from the monstrous absurdity of giving the army half a dozen heads instead of one. The Ordnance alter your barracks, yet I know nothing of it, because we belong to separate armies—one under the Master-General of the Ordnance, the other under the Master-General of the Cavalry and Infantry. Then comes a third, the Master-General of Finance. Last, not least, the Master-General of the Home Office, more potent than all. Besides these, you and I have our little masters-general, the magistrates. God help the poor English army among so many cooks. Were it broth it would have been spoiled long ago." Just fourteen years later the Masters-General and their armies of conflicting clerks were to prove themselves more formidable destroyers of the English army in the Crimea than all the generals and soldiers of the Russian Czar.

The danger being for the moment past, Napier has time to run round his garrisons, and then up to London for twenty-four hours to be invested by the Queen with the Ribbon of the Bath. For many years he has not mixed with or seen his old comrades of Peninsular days; now he meets them at the Palace—alas! "worn, meagre, gray-headed, stooping old men, sinking fast! When we had last been together we were young, active, full of high spirits—dark or auburn locks. Now all are changed, all are parents, all full of cares. Well, the world is chained hand to hand, for there were also young soldiers there, just fledged, meet companions for their young Queen. They too will grow old, but will they have the memory of battles when like us they hurry towards the grave?" Fifty years have gone by, and Time has answered the last query. The fledglings of that day are now white and bent and broken, and when their old eyes gaze into the winter firelight, the

Alma's height, the long valley of Balaklava, the slope of Inkermann, or the snow-clad mounds of the great siege rise before them, even as Corunna and Busaco and Fuentes d'Onoro and the breach at Badajos came back to the older veterans.

The picture given in Napier's journal is one that would have been worth painting, so full of contrast was it, so deep-set in history. "There was our pretty young Queen receiving our homage, and our old shrivelled bodies and gray heads were bowed before her throne, intimating our resolution to stand by it as we had stood when it was less amiably filled. I wonder what she thought of us old soldiers! We must have appeared to her like wild beasts. Lord Hill is old and has lost his teeth, poor Sir John Jones looked like a ghost, and Sir Alexander Dickson is evidently breaking. Thinking how these men had directed the British thunders of war I saw that death was the master. The brilliance of the Court vanished, and the grim spectre stared me in the face. His empire is creeping over all!"

During the summer of 1839 the Chartist agitation went on, and more than once England was on the verge of actual rebellion. Napier's position was a very peculiar one. Thoroughly in sympathy with the people in the objects they had in view, but sternly opposed to any attempt to obtain these objects by force, he ran the danger of falling between the two stools of opinion and duty. He was at this time sailing upon a very dangerous sea, and a single false movement might have involved England in bloodshed. In his letters and reports to his civil and military superiors we find the line ever distinctly drawn between the immediate repression of disorder, which he can answer for at any moment, and the permanent remedy for the evil, which must be the work of the Government. To the military authorities these expressions of opinion on the part of their subordinate appear utterly unprecedented. Napier has told the Commander-in-Chief that he can see no way to meet the evils but to concede to the people their just rights, while the principle of order is at the same time vigorously upheld. The answer to this is suggestive of many thoughts. "Lord Hill desires me to point out your observation and to suggest that you avoid all remarks having allusion to political questions; and I am to say, without entering into the merits of the question, that neither he, as Commander-in-Chief, nor you, as the Major-General commanding the Northern District, can have anything to do with the matter; it is therefore better that you should confine yourselves to what is strictly your provinces as military men." And there is another fact revealed to us in the pages of Napier's correspondence at this time which must strike the reader of to-day as strange. It is told in his account of a public dinner to which he was invited in September, 1839. He had accepted the invitation, thinking it would not be a party demonstration; but he soon found he was mistaken. All the great ones of the county were assembled, with the Lord-Lieutenant in the chair. "Church and State" was the first toast, and it was received with rapturous approval. Then, in the second place, came the health of the Queen. "Glasses were filled," writes Napier, "but not a sound of applause followed. Her Majesty's health was drunk in significant silence. No man cried 'God bless her' except myself. Then came 'The Queen Dowager [the widow of William the Fourth] and the rest of the royal family.' Instantly the room shook with shouts of applause." "You are in the wrong box, General," whispered Napier's right-hand neighbour, one of the members for the county. "So it seems, my lord," answers the irate soldier; "and the reigning Queen is in it too." How strangely this episode reads to-day; yet at the time it was common enough in the ranks of the Tory party. It was only a few years earlier that a widespread conspiracy was afloat among the men who called themselves the True Blues of their party to shut out the Princess Victoria from the throne and substitute the Duke of Cumberland for the succession. How far this conspiracy extended will not perhaps be fully known in our day; but in point of absolute loyalty to the person of the sovereign it is probable that the "rebel" Chartists at the time had a good deal more of it than had some of the supporters of Church and State who were so anxious to shoot them down.

Placed thus between the devil of the classes and the deep sea of the masses it is easy to surmise that Napier had no pleasant berth in this his first command as a general officer. Frequently we find him regretting his refusal of the Australian appointment two years earlier, and picturing to himself a land where men worked in the open air instead of in collieries or factories, a land where taxes were light and people were contented, and the grades of life were not marked by terrible extremes. Here are a few thoughts from his journal, worth in their plain truth and honest judgment many tons weight of the rubbish which the political economists of that time and since have poured forth to the world. "I was mad," he writes in August, 1839, "not to go out as governor of Australia. I could have founded there a great kingdom, with a systematic education, annual parliaments, and the abolition of the law of primogeniture as regards land. I would have so ruled Australia that the land should never have been thus collected." Then he goes on to the question of what constitutes the true prosperity of a nation. "Men," he writes, "are restless and discontented with poverty in manufacturing places. They have all its sufferings and have not those pleasures which make people content under it, that is, health, enjoyment of country life, fresh air, and interest in the seasons and in the various products of nature. The exhausted, unhealthy manufacturer has no such enjoyment; he has no resources but gin, gambling, and all kinds of debauchery. The countryman worships God, the manufacturer worships gold, and thus the practice of sin united to mammon-worship makes the ruffian. Yet such is the system which your political economists call the prosperity of the nation. Hell may be paved with good intentions, but it is assuredly hung with Manchester cottons." As the year 1839 drew to a close, the starvation and misery seemed to deepen over the northern command. In November we read, "The streets of this town [Manchester] are horrible. The poor starving people go about in twenties and forties begging, but without the least insolence; and yet some rich villains and some foolish women choose to say they try to extort charity. It is a lie, an infernal lie; neither more nor less. Nothing can exceed the good behaviour of these poor people, except it be their cruel sufferings." Hard as had been his nine long years of inaction, and welcome as work was to his brain and hand hungry for toil, Napier loathes the employment which carries with it the danger of having to take the lives of his fellow-countrymen. On January 16th, 1840, we find him writing the following entry in his journal: "Anniversary of the battle of Corunna. Oh, that I should have outlived that day to be at war with my own countrymen! Better be dead than live to see a civil war!" In the summer of 1841 a rumour reaches him that he is soon to be offered an Indian command. The old fighting spirit kindles at once in his heart. It will be a pleasant change to the Indus, on the very threshold of the Afghan country where war is raging, from this northern district, where his command is "slavery under noodles." "Gladly shall I get away," he writes, "from this district; for how to deal with violence produced by starvation, by folly, by villainy, and even by a wish to do right, is a hard matter. A man is easily reconciled to act against misled people if he has an honest plan of his own; but if he is only a servant of greater knaves than those he opposes, and feels he is giving strength to injustice, he loses the right stimulus to action."

CHAPTER VIII
INDIA—THE WAR IN SCINDE

When Sir Charles Napier set out for India in the autumn of 1841 he was, in the ordinary sense of the word, an old man. He was sixty years of age. More than forty years earlier he had begun his military career. Thirty-two years had passed since he had fought at Corunna; and since then what a life of action had been his! And yet this little thin figure, with eagle eye and beaked nose, and long hair streaked with white, which for more than forty years seemed to have been a volcano ever in action, had not yet spent the vast stock of vital energy which it started with. Very far from it. After all his wounds and wanderings, his shipwrecks and disasters, his sorrows and sicknesses, his blows and buffetings, here he was starting out for India, far more full of energy than ten out of a dozen ensigns going out from college to begin life.

On December 13th, 1841, Napier first set foot in India. He had come out by the overland route in two months, and looked upon the journey as a marvel of rapidity. It had cost him very dear; and when he landed in Bombay he had exactly two pounds in his pocket, and his bank-account was *nil*. "Had I then died," he writes, "there was not a farthing left for my children," and he was sixty years of age!

When Napier assumed command of the Poonah Division in the end of 1841, our dominion in India had entered upon a very critical stage of its history. Two years before this date we had sent an army into Afghanistan, ostensibly to seat a rival Ameer on the throne of Cabul—in reality to gain a footing in that mountain land. It was an Asiatic copy of Napoleon's invasion of Spain; and although the Afghans had no outside power to help them, the result was much the same as it had been in the Peninsula. There was at first an apparently easy conquest of the country, then a rising of the people, a retreat and surrender of the invaders, followed by fresh invasions carried on with the savage accessories usual where conquest endeavours to legalise its position by calling a people who are rightly struggling in the cause of their freedom "rebels." At this particular moment—the mid-winter of 1841—a great disaster had befallen our arms. The garrison of Cabul, retreating from that place towards the Kyber Pass, had been annihilated in the defiles of Jugdulluck; the general, a few officers, and their wives having alone been saved by surrender. The two civil organisers of the invasion, M'Naughten and Burnes, had been killed, one in Cabul, the other at a conference with Akbar Khan. Sale still held Jellalabad with an Irish battalion; but the Kyber Pass was between him and India, and that defile was in possession of the Afghans. On the western side of Afghanistan our army held Ghuznee, Candahar, and Quetta; but again the Bolan Pass lay between our forces and Upper Scinde, where a small British army was cantoned on the Indus. When the news of these disasters, always magnified by native rumour, reached the countries which still intervened between our real Indian frontier and Afghanistan—Scinde and the Punjaub—signs of ill-concealed satisfaction began to manifest themselves among the princes and peoples of these still semi-independent States. This Afghan expedition had indeed been a wild and foolish venture, and the first blast of misfortune showed at once the full length and breadth of its absurdity. As each succeeding mail from the northern frontier brought to Bombay some fresh development of this critical situation, Napier bent his mind to master the complicated position of affairs; for daily it became more clear to his practised eye that the forces available on the Indian frontier were not adequate to retrieve the military situation, and that sooner or later he would be sent to the theatre of operations. When the crisis becomes really acute, favouritism lowers its front, and genius sees the road clear for action.

And now at last the chance came—the chance of leading an army of his countrymen in battle, the opportunity which he had longed for through all these weary years since that distant day when, writing to his mother from Hythe, he told her that his highest ambition was to live to command British soldiers in the field. That was just forty years ago, and here at last came the long-wished-for boon; but under what changed conditions! "Oh for forty as at Cephalonia," he writes, "when I laughed at eighteen hours' work under a burning sun; now at sixty how far will my carcass carry me? No great distance! Well, to try is glorious! I am hurrying fast towards the end; it will be fortunate to reach it in the hour of victory. Who would be buried by a sexton in a churchyard rather than by an army in the hour of victory?"

In March, 1842, Lord Ellenborough arrived in India as Governor-General. From Madras he wrote to Napier asking the latter to send him a statement of his views with respect to the manner in which the honour of our arms may be most effectually re-established in Afghanistan. The request found Napier prepared. At once a clear and precise plan was forwarded to meet the new Governor-General on his arrival at Calcutta. We must avenge the disasters to our arms, but how? By "a noble, generous, not a vindictive warfare," after which "it might be very practicable to retire from Afghanistan, leaving a friendly people behind us." What a grand type of soldier this! No military executions, no hanging of men whose only fault was a splendid and heroic love of their own land! Truly the dominion based on such old-world chivalry could laugh at the advance of the Russian—it would not need "a scientific frontier" to defend it.

As the year 1842 progressed, the state of Afghanistan still remained critical. In July Candahar and Jellalabad were still our advanced posts, and all the intervening valleys and defiles were in the hands of the Afghans. Behind, in the Punjaub and in Scinde, the spectacle of delay and indecision on the part of our generals was spreading wider the area of disturbance. Clearly some real chief was wanted to hold together all this wavering discontent which was seething from the sources of the Sutlej to the sea at Kurachee. At last the order came to move to Scinde. Napier received it on the anniversary of the battle of the Coa, fought thirty-two years earlier. At first the recollection that he is now in his sixty-first year, and that he has to leave behind him all he holds dear in life to go out to incessant action in a terrible climate, damps his spirit, but he quickly rallies. He will not even depend upon the advice of the "politicals," as he calls the Civil Servants in Scinde, who for once are to be subject to his orders. These men may be useful, he thinks, but that usefulness "cannot be as councillors to a general officer who should have none but his pillow and his courage." And so with these sentiments and a thousand others equally characteristic of indomitable resolution, courage, and self-dependency, he sets out for Scinde on September 3rd, 1842. "Old Oliver's day," he writes; "the day he won Dunbar and Worcester, and the day he died; and a very good day to die on, as good as the second or the fourth—'*a crowning victory*,' strange."

On the evening of the 3rd the *Zenobia* steamed out of Bombay harbour bound for Kurachee. Never did soldier proceed to the scene of action under more terrible conditions. The vessel carried a detachment of two hundred European troops. Scarcely had she put to sea before cholera of the most fatal type broke out among these soldiers. There was but one doctor on board, few medicines, no preparations to meet such a catastrophe. In an hour after the first case appeared many more had been attacked. Night fell. Drenching rain added to the horror. Scarcely were men attacked ere they died in contortions and agony impossible to describe. The beds of the stricken soldiers were laid on deck; and as they died the bodies were instantly cast overboard. All night long this terrible scene went on. When morning dawned twenty-six bodies had been thrown into the sea. For three days this awful scene continued. One-fourth of the entire troops had perished; eighty more men were down on the reeking, filthy deck. It was a time to try the sternest nerve. The worst scene of carnage on the battle-field could be nothing to this awful visitation. At last the port of Kurachee was gained; the flame of the fell disease seemed to have burned itself out; the survivors were got on shore, but a dozen more unfortunates were doomed to perish on land. In eight days sixty-four soldiers—just a third of the entire number embarked—had died; a few sailors, women, and children also perished.

Bad as was this beginning, it did not seem to damp the spirit or dull the energy of the commander. On September 10th he got on shore with his sick and dying. On the 12th he reviews the garrison of Kurachee, and looks to his ammunition and supplies. Before leaving Bombay he had visited the arsenal there, and had discovered some rockets lying in a corner. He had always a fondness for these somewhat erratic engines of war, and he brought them on with him to Scinde. Now at this review he determines to try one or two of them in front of the troops. An artillery officer, an engineer officer, and the General formed a kind of committee for letting off the missile, no one knowing apparently much about it. The second rocket would not go off when lighted; the committee incautiously approached, the rocket exploded, and the General's leg was cut clean across the calf by a sharp splinter of the iron case. This wound laid him up for a few days; but in a week, unable to stand the confinement any longer, he is carried on board a river steamer and proceeds up the Indus. Certainly a bad continuation to a bad beginning this accident. Yet Napier had good reason to hope that whatever else might stop his career it would not be his legs, for in the past, though sorely tried, they had stood to him well. As a boy at Celbridge he had, while leaping a fence, cut the flesh from his leg in a terrible manner; a few years later at Limerick he had smashed the bone while jumping a ditch to secure a dead snipe. Again, at Corunna, a bullet had damaged this unfortunate leg; and here now at Kurachee, thirty-three years later, this rocket has another gash at it. No use; he "will get the snipe" up this great Indus river, as forty-four years ago he got it on the banks of the Shannon.

And now, leaving this old veteran, but ever-young soldier, steaming up the great river by whose shores he is soon to become the central figure in a long series of great events, we will pause a moment to review the chapter of Scindian history which had led up to this moment.

In the year 1836 Afghanistan lay many hundred miles beyond our nearest frontier, and it is almost needless to say that Russia then lay many thousand miles beyond the farthest extreme of Afghanistan. Nevertheless it was determined by the Viceroy of India and his Council to invade Afghanistan across the intervening Sikh and Scindian territory, in order to upset the ruler of the first-named State, and to seat upon the throne of Cabul a king who had long been our puppet and our pensionary. It is of course unnecessary to add that our puppet and our pensionary was, in return for this service, to hand over to us the legs of his throne, the keys of his kingdom, and a good deal of the contents of his treasury. Between our frontier and that of Afghanistan lay the Punjaub and Scinde, through which States we were to invade the territory of Dost Mahomed by the passes of the Khyber and the Bolan. With the ruler of the Punjaub, Runjeet Singh, we were upon terms of closest offensive and defensive amity. He was, in fact, our ally in the invasion. With the rulers of Scinde, on the other hand, our relations were strained. Runjeet was rich, had a large army, and was a single despotic ruler. The Ameers of Scinde were rich too, but they had no regular army. They were fighting among themselves, filled with mutual jealousies, weak rulers of a separated State. The line of policy pursued towards these States by the Calcutta Government was a very obvious if a very flagrant one. Runjeet Singh, the Lion of Lahore, was to be bribed into acquiescence in our Afghan policy, by slices of territory taken from Afghanistan and Scinde, by large promises of plunder to be given him by Shah Soojah, our puppet king, and by subsidies from our own treasury. But with the Ameers of Scinde the process was to be altogether one of force. Pressed by an army on the middle Indus, by the Sikhs from the Punjaub, and by a flotilla on the coast, they were to be squeezed into compliance with our demands, which included cession of territory, fortresses, and seaports, payment of treasure to Shah Soojah, annual subsidies to ourselves, and rights of passage for troops and supplies. All these matters having been arranged to the complete dissatisfaction of the weak but indignant Ameers, our armies pressed on into the Khyber on one hand and the Bolan on the other. This was in 1838. We have already seen the final outcome of this forward Afghan policy in the early months of 1842. That the events in the Koord-Cabul and Jugdulluck Passes, when a single surviving horseman bore to Jellalabad the tidings of a disaster almost unparalleled in the annals of retreating armies, should have been received by the Ameers of Scinde without regret is not to be wondered at, and that they should see in it some opportunity of loosening the grasp of our power upon a territory which we still continued to speak of as independent is equally no subject of astonishment.

When Lord Ellenborough arrived in India in the spring of 1842 he was face to face with immense difficulties. The forward Afghan policy had collapsed. To an ignorant and presumptuous confidence paralysis and fear had succeeded. What was to be done? To reverse the engines and go full speed astern would only run the vessel of Indian policy upon the shoals and quicksands which the former mistaken and most unjust statecraft had produced. Napier knew all this nefarious history when he went to Scinde, but he knew too the utter impossibility of getting again into deep water by a recurrence to an absolutely just policy with the rulers of Scinde. He and his master, Lord Ellenborough, were the inheritors of this trouble. They had not made it, but assuredly they would be measured by it. In India, to go forward has often been to go wrong, but to go back in that country has always been to admit the wrong; and once to do that is to admit the truth of an argument which, if prolonged to its fullest consequences, must lead us to the sea-coast. What then was to be done? Reconquer Afghanistan;

give it up to its old ruler again, and then fix the frontier of India at the frontier of Afghanistan. That was practically the policy determined upon by Lord Ellenborough, and when he made Charles Napier the right arm of its accomplishment he had secured the best pilot then navigating the troubled sea of English dominion in the East.

But when this policy had been once decided on, it would have been better to have openly admitted the necessity, and to have told the Ameers of Scinde plainly our intentions; let them then fight us if they liked. That course would have probably saved a vast effusion of blood. It certainly would have prevented the long and unhappy years of quarrel and recrimination that followed the conquest of Scinde, and the spectacle of two gallant and noble soldiers waging a lifelong war between each other upon the methods by which that conquest had been effected. Of this last phase, however, of the Scindian question we will speak later on.

Steaming up the Indus, Napier reached Hyderabad on September 25th, and had an interview with the Ameers of Scinde. They received him with extraordinary state and honour, for already the tide of war in Afghanistan had turned. Two armies marching from Jellalabad and Candahar had retaken Cabul, and another retiring from the Bolan would soon be on the middle Indus; while a general, of whom fame spoke highly, had just arrived with fresh troops at Kurachee.

Napier passed on from this reception, and early in October arrived at Sukkur, where important letters from Lord Ellenborough reached him; at the same time he received news that the English army had safely passed the Bolan, and that the war in Afghanistan was therefore closed. And now, for the first time in the life of this extraordinary soldier, we arrive at a point where the path is not clear. The situation which at this moment confronted him was perhaps as difficult a one as ever presented itself to a soldier-ruler in our time. The course pursued by Napier was long the subject of fierce controversy. Volumes were written upon it. It was angrily debated in Parliament, angrily commented upon in the Press, and as angrily defended and applauded on the other side. All this is long over; the heat, the fury, and the bitter words have passed with the generation that saw and read in the flesh of the doings on the Indus. The conquest of Scinde has taken its place in history, and we can now quietly estimate the difficulties, the rights, the wrongs, and what perhaps was stranger than all, the temptations of the time. We will lightly touch upon them all, remembering that our path lies upon the ashes of dead heroes. First for the situation. It was this. A great shock had just been given to the sagacity of British government in India, and what was more important, to the prestige of British arms in Asia. We had retreated from Afghanistan, after avenging our defeat it is true, but still by the fact of that retreat acknowledging that our policy had been wrong, and that our power of enforcing that policy had not been equal to its ambition. That was a very serious position for a power whose dominion in the East rested solely on the sword, and nowhere was it so serious as in the neutral borderlands through which we had passed in order to invade Afghanistan—the lands whose natural rights we had trenched upon, and whose sentiments of independence we had repeatedly outraged during the five years of this unfortunate enterprise. Now one fact was very clear to the Viceroy in Calcutta and to his lieutenant in Scinde—either we must withdraw altogether from the Indus, or we must strengthen our position there. The first course was altogether out of the question, the second became a necessity. Lord Ellenborough directed Napier to draft a new treaty, told him to present it to the Ameers, and if necessary to enforce its acceptance by arms. So far all was clear. In November, 1842, the new treaty was ready for presentation to the Ameers. Its provisions were indeed formidable. It took from the rulers of Scinde, towns, territory, rights of coinage, etc., and it especially dealt severely with the northern or Khyrpoor Ameers, who were rightly or wrongly suspected of having been desirous of profiting by the Afghan disasters in the preceding year. Two men of a widely different character appear at this moment upon the scene—Major James Outram of the Indian army, now political agent in Scinde, and His Highness Ali Moorad, one of the Ameers of Khyrpoor. No braver soldier ever bore the arms of England in the East than James Outram. No baser intriguer ever schemed and plotted for his own advancement than Ali Moorad of northern Scinde. Napier presented his treaty to the Ameers, and at the same time moved his troops into the territory the cession of which was claimed by the document. The Ameers accepted the treaty, but protested against its severity. The leading Ameer was a very old man, over eighty years of age, named Meer Roostum. Between him and his younger half-brother, Ali Moorad, lay a great gap of years—perhaps forty—and a still greater gap of hatred, for Ali longed to possess his elder brother's lands, rights, and *puggaree*, as the turban, or insignia of paramount power, was called. Outram was anxious to save the Ameers from the total destruction which he knew must await them if arms were made the arbitrament of the dispute. Ali Moorad saw that only by a recourse to war could his scheme of ambition be gratified. Between them stood Napier, determined upon using to the utmost the immense power which the Viceroy had placed in his hands, and seeing far beyond the present dispute a time when this valley of the Indus must all become British territory; seeing it in imagination, too, a happy valley waving with grain, peopled by a peaceful and contented population free from the exactions of semi barbarian chiefs, and enjoying the blessings of a government which would rule them with patriarchal justice—a picture the reality of which no human eye has ever looked on.

But above and beyond all this there was another spring in Charles Napier's mind, more potent than any picture, more powerful than any prompting. Above everything else he was a soldier. The clash of arms was dear to him as music to the ear of an Italian. No lover ever longed for mistress more than did this man long for fighting. Was he bloodthirsty? Not in the least. His heart was tender as a child's, his sympathies were far-reaching as a woman's; but for all that every fibre of his nature vibrated to the magic touch of military glory, and his earthly paradise was the front rank of battle.

That his soldier nature was all this time in a state of antagonism with the other nature of pity and love of abstract justice cannot be doubted for a moment. The conflict peeps out through hundreds of pages of his journals. How glad he would be if these Ameers would boldly reject the treaty and defy him! "I almost wish," he writes on December 5th, "that they proudly defied us and fought, for they are so weak, so humble, that punishing them goes against the grain." Most men who read his life to-day will echo that regret. All this while the unfortunate Ameers, divided by conflicting counsels, and distracted by the rumours of coming war which Ali Moorad industriously circulated among them, were drifting rapidly to ruin. The older men were for complete submission, the younger hands were advising resistance. The wild Beloochee matchlock men and the fierce horsemen of Scinde were clamorous not to allow the old fame of the Talpoors to die out in shameful surrender. The Feringhee, even when the treaty had been signed, would move on Hyderabad. The treasure of the Ameers was great, their harems were numerous. If they were doomed to lose all, better lose all with arms in their hands facing the invader. Such was the state of affairs during the month of December, 1842. The Ameers are irresolute and distracted by a thousand reports; Ali Moorad is deeply scheming to make Napier believe his relatives mean fighting; Outram, the Ameers' best friend, has been sent by Lord Ellenborough away from Scinde, and at Napier's request is about to return from Bombay; and Napier himself, dazzled with the realisation of his life-long dream of military glory, is about "to cut with the sword the Gordian knot" of Scindian politics. In the middle of the month of December he crossed his army from the right to the left bank of the Indus at Sukkur, and put his troops in column of route. The state of his mind at this moment is laid bare to us in his journal; on December 21st he writes thus:

> Ten thousand fighting men and their followers are camped here at Alore, a town built by Alexander the Great. My tent overlooks this most beautiful encampment. The various sounds, the multitude of followers, the many costumes and languages, and the many religions, produce a strange scene which makes a man think, Why is all this?

Why am I supreme? A little experience in the art of killing, of disobedience to Heaven's behests, is all the superiority that I, their commander, can boast of! How humbled thinking makes me feel! Still, I exult when beholding this force. I have worked my way to this great command, and am gratified at having it, yet despise myself for being so gratified! Yes, I despise myself, not as feeling unworthy to lead, for I am conscious of knowing how to lead, and my moral and physical courage are equal to the task; my contempt is for my worldliness. Am I not past sixty? Must I not soon be on the bed of death? And yet so weak as to care for these things. No, I do not. I pray to do what is right and just, and to have strength to say, 'Get thee behind me, Satan.' Alas, I have not the strength! Well, this comfort remains—with a secret and strong desire to guide in war, I have avoided it studiously!

At four o'clock in the morning following Christmas Day he put his troops in motion for the south. On the last night of the year he is encamped near Khyrpoor; to his right lies the level alluvial valley of the Indus, to his left the great desert of Scinde rolls away in measureless sand-waves. Walking in front of his tent and looking at the long line of camp fires, while the hum of his host floats up through the glorious Eastern night, he begins as it were to speak his thoughts aloud. All his plans are formed. "One night," he says, "I drank strong coffee and had a capital *think* for an hour. I got many matters decided in that hour." He will march first into the desert on his left and take the fort of Emanghur, a stronghold of the northern Ameers of high repute because it is an island in a waterless sea; then will come back to the Indus and direct his march upon Hyderabad. The Ameers will fly, he thinks, across the Indus, and the entire left bank of the river from the Punjaub to the sea will become British territory. If the Ameers elect to fight, well, he will be glad to give them every opportunity. "Peace and civilisation will then replace war and barbarism. My conscience will be light, for I see no wrong in so regulating a set of tyrants who are themselves invaders, and have in sixty years nearly destroyed the country. The people hate them. I may be wrong, but I cannot see it, and my conscience will not be troubled. I sleep well while trying to do this, and shall sleep sound when it is done." Here in these few words we have the picture of the invasion of Scinde as he then saw it. Nevertheless it was not the picture which India saw, which Outram saw, and which calm and impartial history must see to-day. And here let us look for a moment on the field of war, for war it was to be, that lay before this army camped under the winter starlight on this last night of 1842.

A vast dreary world was this Scinde. Men who knew it best called it the Unhappy Valley, and the name fitted accurately the nation. A flat, dusty, sun-scorched, fever-poisoned land; an Egypt turned the wrong way, and with a past so blurred and battered that no eye could read it; a changeless landscape of dusty distance through which the meanest habitations of men loomed at intervals, with ragged solitary acacia trees, and old broken mosques and mounds that had once been cities, and towns that were always shrinking, and graveyards that were ever growing. In the centre of this Unhappy Valley rolled the Indus—a broad rapid river when the summer flood poured down its silt-sided channel, a lean shrunken stream when winter heaped high his snowflakes in the mountains of Afghanistan; and yet a rich land wherever water could be given to its thirsty surface. Man had only to scuffle and hoe the baked dust, pour water over it, and in a month or two the arid plain became a waving sea of emerald green, to quickly change again to a vast level of yellowing grain. But it is a strange fact that wherever these conditions of dusty desert turned green with animal inundation are found, there too you will find man a slave and a tyrant. Grades there may be between, but always the lowest layers of the human strata will be slaves, and the upper ones will be their owners. And nowhere was this rule more certain than in Scinde. The native Scindian who grubbed the earth, dug the canal, and turned the water-wheel, was a slave. The Beloochee, whether he called himself predatory hill-man, settled lord of the valley, or ruling Ameer, was a tyrant. What the Mameluke had been to Egypt the Beloochee was to Scinde—a ruling caste, fierce fighters, making free with every rule of their prophet, faithful only to his fanatic spirit. Three separate groups of rulers called Ameers governed Scinde. They all claimed equal descent from the Talpoor chief who, seventy years before this period, had come down from Beloochistan and conquered the Unhappy Valley. There were the Ameers of Lower Scinde, who dwelt in Hyderabad; those of Upper Scinde, whose headquarters was Khyrpoor; and those of East Scinde, who ruled at Meerpoor. As their descent was equal, so their characters were alike. Prosperity and power and self-indulgence had taken the old Beloochee steel out of their natures. They drank, they feasted, they hunted, and they loved after the fashion of the East. That they were not so weak or so vicious as a thousand rulers of India lying farther south is clear, but it was only because they were nearer to the mountains from whose flinty rocks they had come three generations earlier. Everything that has ever descended from these grim northern hills has degenerated in India. The Arab fares no better than does his horse when once he passes those arid portals.

Such was the land and such the people with whom Napier was now to come to blows in the new year about to dawn. War had not been declared, but it was certain that some of the Ameers at least were gathering their

Beloochee feudatories, that it was often stated in their durbars that the hot season, now near at hand, would paralyse the action of the English general, and that, as a bold and resolute front had ended in Afghanistan in the total withdrawal of the English armies, so might that most necessary adjunct to the string of diplomacy ensure the final retirement of the Feringhee from the territories of Scinde. Ever present in Napier's mind was this approaching hot season. Viewing the conduct of the principal Ameers through the glasses of his new friend and ally, Meer Ali Moorad, and seeing with his own eyes the evidence of their tyrannical rule over their subjects, he had resolved to anticipate all plans, to forestall all projects, to determine all events by marching at once upon the chief strongholds of the Ameers. If his innate love of justice whispered to him any suggestion that the cause of quarrel was not clear, that the chief Ameers were divided among themselves, and that moderate counsels would prevail over their fears and their weakness, the spectacle of their tyranny and worthlessness, of Beloochee bloodthirstiness and Scindian slavery, was ever before his vision to shut out such misgivings. The government of the Ameers seemed in his eyes as monstrous and unjust as had the Irish government of his boyish days or the English administration of Castlereagh and Sidmouth, and all the pent torrent of his nature longed to go out and crush it. Love of glory, hatred of oppression, these two most potent factors in the story of his life, called him to the field; he forgot that it is possible to be unjust even to injustice, and that if there were no criminals there need be no mercy.

On January 5th, 1843, he struck out with a small force for the desert fortress of Emanghur.

CHAPTER IX
THE BATTLE OF MEANEE

The desert—the world before it was born or after its death, the earth without water, no cloud above, no tree below—space, silence, solitude, all realised in one word—there is nothing like it in creation.

At midnight on January 5th the little column started for Emanghur,—three hundred and fifty men of the Twenty-Second Regiment on camels—two men on each—two twenty-four pounders drawn by camels, and two hundred troopers of the Scinde Horse, with fifteen days' food and four days' water. From a group of wells called Choonka, Napier sent back a hundred and fifty of his horse, and pushed on with the remainder. For seven days he held on through the sea of sand, and on the 12th reached his object. It was deserted by the Beloochees, who had abandoned their redoubtable stronghold at the approach of the British. On the last day's march the men of the Twenty-Second had to dismount from their camels and help to drag the heavy howitzer through the sand, all laughing and joking, and with such strength! We shall see these men a few weeks later doing still more splendid work, and will have a few words to say about them; now we must hurry on. Napier blew up the desert fort and turned his face back towards the Indus. On January 16th he is still toiling through the sand waves, the men again dragging the guns, but with a significant absence of laughter now that the chances of fight are over. It is the anniversary of Corunna, and despite the labour and anxieties which surround him, the General's mind is away in the past. He reviews the long career now stretching like this desert into an immense horizon. In this retrospect his mind fastens upon one satisfactory thought—he and his brothers have not disgraced their father's memory. "We all resolved not to disgrace him," he writes, "and were he now alive he would be satisfied." The previous day, with the tremendous explosion of the blowing up of Emanghur still ringing in his ears, he wrote: "All last night I dreamed of my beloved mother; her beauteous face smiled upon me. Am I going to meet her very soon?" No, they were not to meet soon; for in spite of fierce battle and Scindian sun and life long past its prime, he is still to realise in himself that mysterious promise given in even a vaster desert than this to those who hold dear the memory of father and mother—he will be left long in the land he is soon to conquer.

By the end of January he has cleared the desert, reunited his column to the main body, and turned the head of his advance to the south. All this time negotiations were going on. Outram had gone to Hyderabad. The Ameers were in wildest confusion; they would sign anything one day, on the next it was protest, threat, or supplication. Camel and horse messengers were flying through the land. But amid all this varying mass of diplomatic rumour one fact was certain, the Ameers' fighting feudatories were gathering, the wild sword and matchlock men of the hills and the deserts were assembling at Hyderabad. The last day of January had come. In another month or six weeks the terrible sun would be hanging as a blazing furnace overhead, and it would be too late. "If they would turn out thirty thousand men in my front it would relieve me from the detestable feeling of having to deal with poor miserable devils that cannot fight, and are seeking pardon by submission. Twenty times a day I am forced to say to myself, 'Trust them not; they are all craft; be not softened.'" Halting five days at Nowshara to allow further time for negotiations and to rest his own troops, he resumes his march early in February. He is at Sukurunda on the 10th, and here again he halts for some days; for Outram has written from Hyderabad that the Ameers have accepted the treaty, and he prays a further respite. But at this place an event occurred which did much to decide the wavering balance between peace and war. On the night of February 12th Napier's cavalry seized some Beloochee chiefs passing the left of the camp. They were of the Murree hill tribe, and the leader of the clan, Hyat Khan, was among them. On him was found a letter from Ameer Mahomet of Hyderabad calling upon him to assemble all his warriors and to march to Meanee on the 9th. The discovery of this message at once decided Napier. He would march straight to his front; he would attack whatever barred his road, be they six or sixty thousand. The events that happened in these early days of February, 1843, and the trembling balance which now was decided to the side of war, have been made the occasion of long and fierce controversy. Volumes were written on Napier's side and on Outram's side. Did the Ameers mean war all the time, and were their professions of peace only directed to delay events until their soldiers were collected and the hot season had come? Or were they a poor helpless lot of enervated rulers, driven to resist the aggression of the English general, and only fighting at last when every other avenue of settlement had been closed against them? To us now two things are very clear. First, that Napier played the game of negotiation with the Ameers from first to last with an armed hand, ready to strike if there was hesitation on the part of his adversaries. Second, that his adversaries played precisely the same game with him. Both sides got their fighting men out. One began its march, the other took up its position of defence. That the flint on one side and the steel on the other, represented by their respective fighting forces, were anxious to come to blows there cannot be a doubt; and that when they found themselves only a few marches distant from each other they struck and fire flew, need never have been the cause of wonderment, least of all the cause of wonderment to soldiers. And now for the clash of flint and steel which bears the name of the battle of Meanee.

From the village of Hala, thirty-three miles north of Hyderabad, two roads led to that city. One of these, that nearer the Indus, approached the position of Meanee directly in front; the other, more to the east, turned that place on its right. Napier reached Hala on the morning of the 18th, and there his mind became immovably determined. In the afternoon Outram arrived by steamer from Hyderabad, having been attacked on the previous day in the Residency by a division of the Beloochee army, with six guns. He had successfully resisted the attack with his small force for some hours, but, finding his ammunition running short, he withdrew with the little garrison to his steamers. There could now be no further doubt that the Ameers had elected to appeal to the sword, and the path was at last clear before Napier and his army. He will advance along the road nearest to the river; if possible he will manœuvre to turn the enemy's right when he is face to face with him. "There is but one thing—battle!" he writes on this day. "Had Elphinstone fought, he would not have lost his character. Had Wellington waited for Stevenson at Assaye, he would have been beaten. Monson hesitated and retreated and was beaten." Then he pushed on to Muttaree, one march from the Beloochee position. At this place, Muttaree, many things happened. During the day and night various reports came in as to the strength of the enemy. Outram says they are eighteen thousand strong, the spies report twenty to twenty-five, and thirty thousand Beloochees in position. They are flocking in so fast to Meanee that in another day or two there may be sixty thousand assembled. "Let them be sixty or one hundred thousand," is his reply, "I will fight." All the arrangements for the advance are now made. He will move his little army—it is only twenty-two hundred strong—after midnight, so as to arrive in front of Meanee by nine o'clock next morning. Then he sits down to write his letters and bring up his journal to date; for this coming battle, which is to be his first essay as Commander-in-Chief, may be his last as a soldier. "To fall will be to leave many I love," he writes to his old and true friend John Kennedy; "but to go to many loved, to my home! and that in any case must be soon"; for is he not sixty-one years of age? Then, having written all his letters and closed his journal with a message to his wife and children, which shows how the grand heart of the man was ever torn by love and steeled by duty, he goes out of his hut to visit the outposts and see that all is safe in the sleeping camp. It is now midnight. He lies down—has three hours' sleep, and at three A.M. the fall-in sounds and the march to Meanee begins.

When day dawns the column is within a few miles of the enemy. The road leads over a level plain of white silt with a few stunted bushes growing at intervals upon it. To the right and left of this plain, extensive woods close the view. These *shikargahs* (hunting preserves) are about three-quarters of a mile apart, and the intervening plain across which the road leads is here and there seared by a *nullah* or dry watercourse. Clouds of dust rise into the morning air from the feet of horses, men, camels, and the roll of wheels.

When there is good light to see, the halt is sounded and the men breakfast; then the march is resumed, and in another hour the leading scouts are in sight of the enemy. It is now eight o'clock. The enemy seems to occupy a deep and sudden depression in the plain on a front of twelve hundred yards, extending right across the line of advance and touching the woods on each flank. Before his right flank there is a village which he also occupies, but no other obstacle lies between the British advancing column and the great hollow in which the Beloochee line of battle has been formed. Napier halts his advanced guard, and while awaiting the arrival of his main body, still a considerable distance in rear, endeavours to obtain some idea of the enemy's strength and position. It is no easy matter. The woods to right and left hide whatever troops he has on these flanks, and the deep *nullah* in front conceals his strength in that direction; but beyond the *nullah*, where the plain resumes its original level, the morning sun strikes upon thousands of bits of steel, and a vague dust hanging overhead tells of a vast concourse of human beings on the earth below it.

When the column arrives in line with the advanced guard there is a busy interval getting the immense baggage-train into defensive position, pushing forward guns and cavalry, deploying the infantry into line of battle, and trying to obtain from the top of some sand-dune a better view of the enemy's position. When all is ready for the final advance across the last thousand yards, one thing is certain to the General,—there is no chance of manœuvring to gain the Beloochee flank. The woods are too dense, *nullahs* intersect them, they swarm with the enemy—there is nothing possible but to attack the centre straight in front across the bare white plain. There is a small mud village before the enemy's right flank, where the left *shikargah* touches the bank of the big hollow. The nearer bank of this big hollow has a slight incline towards the plain, and above its level edge many heads can be seen through the field-glasses, and tall matchlock-barrels are constantly moving along it. This hollow is in fact the bed of the Fullalee river, a deep channel which quits the main stream of the Indus three or four miles farther to the right and bends round here to the village of Meanee, where, making a sudden turn to the south, it bends back towards Hyderabad. It is a flowing river only when the Indus is in flood; now the Indus is low and the Fullalee is a deep wide water-course destitute of water, or holding it only in a few stagnant pools. It is in this dry river-bed that the main portion of the Beloochee army is drawn up, and beyond it, in a loop of level ground which the river-channel makes between its bend, can be seen the tents and camp-equipage of the chiefs whose clansmen are arrayed beneath.

Carrying the glass still to the right along the nearer edge of the dry channel, the eye noted that the *shikargah*, or jungle-cover, which formed the left of the Beloochee army had a high wall dividing it from the plain, and that about midway between the enemy and the British line a large gap or opening had been made in this formidable obstacle. In an instant the quick eye of the General noted this opening. It was the gate of a proposed trap. Through it the left wing of the enemy would debouch upon the rear of the British when the little army would have passed the spot to engage the centre in the Fullalee. In the angles formed by the *shikargahs* where they touched the Fullalee there were six guns in battery, while the entire front of the Beloochee position for a distance of some seven hundred yards had been cleared of even the stunted trees which elsewhere grew upon the plain. All these things Charles Napier took in in that short and anxious interval which preceded the final advance of his little army. It was not a sight that longer examination could make more pleasant. It was a strong and well-selected position, taken up with care and foresight, not to be turned on either flank, forcing the enemy that would attack it to show his hand at once, while it kept hidden from that assailant and safe from his shot, the main body of its defenders.

And now the British line of battle has reached to within nine hundred yards of this strong position which we have just glanced along. Let us see in what manner of military formation the English General moves his men to attack it. Line, of course; for every memory of his old soldier life held some precious moment consecrated to the glory of the red line of battle. Thirty years had rolled over him since he had seen that glorious infantry moving in all the splendour of its quiet courage to the shock of battle. Many things had changed since then, but the foot soldier was still the same. Now as in Peninsular days he came mostly from those lowly peasant homes which greed and foolish laws had not yet levelled with the ground. Now as in Peninsular days he was chiefly Irish. When Napier rode at the head of his marching column in Scinde, when he chatted as he loved to do at the halt or in the camp with the "man in the ranks," the habit of thought and mode of expression were the same as they had been in the far-off marches and bivouacs by the Tagus or the Coa. True, in this Scindian strife he had only a single regiment of that famous infantry in his army. But that single regiment was worth a host. "I have one British regiment," he had written only the previous night, "the Twenty-Second, magnificent Tipperary! I would not give your *specimens* for a deal just now." What manner of men these Tipperary soldiers were, Sir William Napier tells us in his *Conquest of Scinde*. The description is worth repeating, because the picture is rarer than it used

- 74 -

to be. "On the left of the artillery," he writes, describing the advance to Meanee, "marched the Twenty-Second Regiment. This battalion, about four hundred in number, was composed almost entirely of Irishmen, strong of body, high-blooded, fierce, impetuous soldiers who saw nothing but victory before them, and counted not their enemies." On the left of the Twenty-Second Regiment marched four battalions of native infantry, resolute soldiers moving with the firm tread which discipline so easily assumes when it is conscious of being led by capacity and courage. In front of the line of infantry thus formed, the Scinde Horse on the left and the grenadier and light companies of the Twenty-Second Regiment were thrown forward for the double purpose of screening the movement of the main body in their rear and of drawing the fire and thereby revealing the position of the enemy in front. With this advanced line of skirmishers rides the General in blue uniform, and conspicuous from the helmeted head-dress which he wears. The soldiers are in the old red coatee with white lappels and forage caps covered with white cotton, for there was no light Karkee clothing or helmets of pith or cork in those days, and the British infantry marched under the sun of India clad almost in the military costume of an English winter.

When the skirmishers reach the large gap in the *shikargah* wall before mentioned, the perfect soldier nature of Napier shows itself—the instant adaptation of means to end which marks the man who has to do his thinking on horseback and amid the whistle of bullets, from the man who has to do it in an easy chair and at an office-table. The wide gap in the high wall has been recently made. It will be used to attack the right rear of our line when engaged in front at the edge of the Fullalee. He will block up this gap with the grenadiers of the Twenty-Second. He will close this gaping wound in his plan of battle with these stalwart Celts, who, he knows, will stop it with their blood. So the grenadiers are closed upon their right flank, wheeled to the right, and pushed into the opening. "He is a good man in a gap" had been a favourite saying among these soldiers when they were peasant lads at home to designate a stout-hearted comrade. They are to prove its truth now.

So, with the grenadier company standing in the gap on his right, his baggage parked in rear, with the camels tied down in a circle, heads inward, forming a rampart around it, and having an escort as strong as he could spare from his already attenuated front, Napier passes on to the assault, all the swords of his cavalry and the bayonets of his infantry just numbering eighteen hundred, while his enemy in the hollow and the woods reckons not a man less than thirty thousand chiefs and clansmen.

And now as the line of *échelon* gets closer to the hollow the fire from matchlock and gun hits harder into the ranks of men moving in the old fighting formation, the red line of battle—thin, men have called it, but very thick for all that, with the memories of many triumphs. The leading line— the Twenty-Second Regiment—is only one hundred yards from the enemy. The moment had come for the skirmishers to fall back and give place to the chief combatants now so near each other. Napier puts himself in front of the Irishmen whose serried line of steel and scarlet extends two hundred yards from right to left, and then the command to charge rings out in his clear voice as three-and-thirty years earlier it sounded above the strife of Corunna. Until this moment the fire of the skirmishers has partly hidden the movement of formations behind; but when the magic word which flings the soldier on his enemy was heard, there came out of this veiling smoke a sight that no Beloochee warrior had ever seen before, for, bending with the forward surge of a mighty movement, the red wall of the Twenty-Second, fronted with steel, is coming on to the charge. It took little time to traverse the intervening space, and on the edge of the dry river-bed the two opposing forces met in battle. If to the Beloochee foeman the sight and sound of a British charge had been strange, not less terrible was the aspect of the field, as all at once it opened upon the Twenty-Second. Below them, in the huge bed of the Fullalee, a dense dark mass of warriors stood ready for the shock. With flashing swords and shields held high over turbaned heads, twenty thousand men shouting their war-cries and clashing sword and shield together seemed to wave fierce welcome to their enemies. For a moment it seems as though the vast disparity between the combatants must check the ardour of the advancing line; for a moment the red wall appears to stagger, but then the figure of the old General is seen pushing out in front of his soldiers, as with voice and gesture, and the hundred thoughts that find utterance at moments of extreme tension, he urges them to stand steady in this terrible combat. And nobly do these young soldiers—for this is their first battle—respond to the old leader's call. A hundred times the Beloochee clansmen, moving from the deep mass beneath, come surging up the incline, until from right to left the clash of scimitar and shield against bayonet and musket rings along the line, and a hundred times they reel back again, leaving the musket and the matchlock to continue the deadly strife until another mass of chosen champions again attempts the closer conflict. More than once the pressure of the foremost swordsmen and the appearance of the dense dark mass behind them cause the line of the Twenty-Second to recoil from the edge of the bank; but wherever the dinted front of fight is visible there too is quickly seen the leader, absolutely unconscious of danger, his eagle eye fixed upon the strife, his hand waving his soldiers on, his shrill clear voice ringing above shot and steel and shout of combatants—the clarion call of victory. The men behind him see in this figure of their chief something that hides from sight the whole host of Beloochee foemen. Who could go back while he is there? Who among them would not glory to die with such a leader? The youngest soldier in the ranks feels the inspiration of such magnificent courage. The bugler of the Twenty-Second, Martin Delaney, who runs at the General's stirrups, catches, without necessity of order, the thought of his chief, and three times when the line bends back before the Beloochee onslaught, the "advance" rings out unbidden from his lips.

The final advance to the edge of the Fullalee, which brought the lines to striking distance, had been made in what is called *échelon* of battalions from the right. That is to say, the Twenty-Second Regiment struck the enemy first, then the Twenty-Fifth Sepoys came into impact, and so on in succession until the entire line formed one continuous front along the bank of the dry river. The advantages of this method of assault were many. First, it allowed the Twenty-Second Regiment to give a lead to the entire line, for each succeeding battalion could see with what a front and bearing these splendid soldiers carried themselves in the charge. Then, too, it enabled each particular regiment to come into close quarters with the enemy upon a more regular and imposing front than had the advancing force formed a single line necessarily crowded and undulating by the exigencies of marching in a long continuous formation, and also it made the assault upon the enemy's left flank the last to come to shock of battle; for on this left flank the village of Meanee was held in advance of the river line, and the Beloochee guns in battery there had to be silenced before his infantry could be encountered.

We have already said that our own artillery moved on the extreme right of the infantry. Early in the action they closed up to the right flank of the Twenty-Second, and coming into action on a mound which there commanded the bed of the Fullalee, the farther bank of the river, and the wooded *shikargah* to the right, made havoc among the Beloochee centre on one side, and, on the other, among the left wing which was destined to fall upon our rear. Stopped by the grenadier company from issuing through the large gap in the wall, and taken in flank by two of the guns behind the mound, firing case-shot through another opening in the wall made by the Madras Sappers, this left wing of the enemy suffered so severely that it was unable to make any head. Napier had told the grenadier company to defend the opening to the last man, and nobly did they answer his behest. The captain of the company, Tew, died at his post, but no enemy passed the gap that day.

Meanwhile the fight on the edge of the dry channel went on with a sameness of fierceness that makes its recital almost monotonous. In no modern battle that we read of is the actual shock of opposing forces more than a question of a few moments' duration. Here at Meanee it is a matter of hours. For upwards of three hours this red line is fighting that mass of warriors at less than a dozen yards' distance, and often during the long conflict the interval between the combatants is not half as many feet. Over and over again heroic actions are performed in that limited area between the hosts that read like a page from some dim combat of Homeric legend. The commander of the Twenty-Fifth Bombay Sepoys, Teesdale, seeing the press of foemen in front of his men to be more than his line can stand, spurs into the midst of the surging mass, and falls, hewing his enemies to the last. But his spirit seems to have quitted his body only to enter into the three hundred men who have seen him fall, and the wavering line bears up again. So, too, when the Sepoy regiment next in line has to bear the brunt of the Beloochee charge, the commanding officer, Jackson, rides forward into the advancing enemy and goes down amid a whirl of sword-blades, his last stroke crashing through a shield vainly raised to save its owner's life, and beats back the Beloochee surge. M'Murdo of the Twenty-Second, riding as staff-officer to the General, cannot resist the intoxication of such combats. Seeing a chief conspicuous alike by martial bearing and richness of apparel, he rides into the enemy's ranks and engages him in single combat. Before they can meet M'Murdo's horse is killed, but the rider is quickly on his feet, and the combat begins. Both are dexterous swordsmen, and each seems to recognise in the other a foeman worthy of his steel; but the Scottish clansman is stouter of sword than his Beloochee rival, and Jan Mahomet Khan rolls from his saddle to join the throng which momentarily grows denser on the sandy river-bed.

Once or twice the old General is himself in the press of the fight. He is practically unarmed, because his right hand had been disabled a few days earlier by a blow which he had dealt a camel-driver who was maltreating his camel, and the Scindian's head being about fifty times harder than the General's hand, a dislocated wrist was the result. So intent is he on the larger battle that the men around him are scarcely noticed, and more than once his life is saved by a soldier or an officer interposing between him and an enemy intent on slaying the old chief, who seems to him exactly what he is—the guiding spirit of this storm of war. Thus Lieutenant Marston saves his General's life in front of the Twenty-Fifth Sepoys by springing between a Beloochee soldier and Napier's charger at the moment the enemy is about to strike. The blow cuts deep into the brass scales on Marston's shoulder, and the Beloochee goes down between the sword of the officer and the bayonet of a private who has run in to the *melée*. Again he gets entangled in the press in front, and is in close peril when a sergeant of the Twenty-Second saves him; and as the old man emerges unscathed from the surf of shield and sword, the whole Twenty-Second line shouts his name and greets him with a wild Irish cheer of rapture ringing high above the clash of battle. It is at this time that the drummer Delaney, who keeps everywhere on foot beside his General, performs the most conspicuous act of valour done during the day. In the midst of the *melée* he sees a mounted chief leading on his men. Delaney seizes a musket and bayonet, rushes upon the horseman, and Meer Wullee Mahomet Khan goes down in full sight of both armies, while the victor returns with the rich sword and shield of the Beloochee leader.

There are no revolvers yet, no breechloading arms, nothing but the sword for the officer and the flint musket and bayonet for the men; and fighting means something more than shoving cartridges in at one end of a tube and blowing them out at the other, twenty to the minute, by the simple action of pulling a finger. "At Meanee," says M'Murdo, "the muskets of the men often ceased to go off, from the pans becoming clogged with powder, and then you would see soldiers, taking advantage of a momentary lull in the onslaught, wiping out the priming pans with a piece of rag, or fixing a new flint in the hammer." Sometimes these manifold inducements to old "brown Bess" to continue work have to be suspended in order to receive on levelled bayonets a wild Beloochee rush, and then frequently could be seen the spectacle of men impaled upon the steel, still hacking down the enemy they had been able to reach only in death.

This desperate battle has continued for three hours, when for the first time the Beloochees show symptoms of defeat. The moment has in fact come which in every fight marks the turn of the tide of conflict, and quick as thought Napier seizes its arrival. His staff officers fly to the left carrying orders to the Scinde Horse and the Bengal Cavalry to penetrate at all hazards through the right of the enemy's line, and fall upon his rear. The orders are well obeyed, and soon the red turbans of Jacob's Horse and the Bengal Cavalry are seen streaming through the Fullalee, and, mounting the opposite slope where the Beloochee camp is pitched, they capture guns, camp, standards, and all the varied insignia of Eastern war. The battle of Meanee is won. Then, beginning with the Twenty-Second, there went up a great cheer of victory. How those Tipperary throats poured forth their triumph, as bounding forward, the men so long assailed became assailants, and driving down the now slippery incline they bore back in quickening movement the wavering mass of swordsmen! Perhaps there was something in that Irish cheer that told the old General there was the note of love as well as of pride in the ring. Why not? Had he not always stood up for them and for their land? Had not their detractors ever been his enemies? Had not he dammed back the tide of his own success in life by championing their unfashionable cause? Soldiers catch quickly thoughts and facts that come to other men through study and reflection.

They were proud of him, they loved him, and for more than half a century their valour and their misfortunes had touched the springs of admiration and sorrow in his heart. How he valued these cheers on the field of Meanee his journal of the following day tells. "The Twenty-Second gave me three cheers after the fight, and one during it," he writes. "Her Majesty has no honour to give that can equal that." What a leader! What soldiers!

CHAPTER X
THE MORROW OF MEANEE—THE ACTION AT DUBBA

Exhausted by the prolonged strain of mind and body—"ready to drop," he tells us, "from the fatigue of one constant cheer"—Napier lay down in his cloak that night in the midst of the dead and dying. Terrible had been the slaughter. More than twelve hundred dead lay in the dry bed of the river immediately in front of where the British line had fought. The woods and surrounding ground held a vast number of bodies. It is estimated that not less than six or seven thousand Beloochees perished in the battle. On our own side the loss, though severe, was slight compared with that of the enemy. About two hundred and seventy of all ranks had been killed and wounded—more than one-seventh of the total number engaged. Of these, nineteen were officers—a third of the number on the ground. These figures give us a good measure of the fierce nature of the struggle, and of the bravery displayed on both sides; but the true lesson of such heroism was not noticed at the time, or rather was kept steadily out of sight by all save a few men, and that lesson was this, that good and courageous leadership means brave and victorious soldiers, and that bad leadership means cowardice and defeat. It was but a year before this day of heroes at Meanee that there had been whole days and weeks of cowardice at Cabul. Infantry, cavalry, artillery; arms, powder, and shot—all the same, yet all the difference between victory and defeat, between honour and dishonour in the two results. It was this fact above every other that caused the display of envious enmity from so many quarters towards Napier and his victory; the contrast was too glaring, the youngest soldier in the ranks could read it. But a year ago the world had beheld the most dishonourable and inglorious chapter of our military history enacted near the head waters of this same Indus river, and here, now, another hand playing the game with the self-same cards had won it against greater odds and braver enemies.

But if it was unpleasant in England to find the lesson of victory taught so well by one who had ever opposed privilege, whether it called itself Whig or Tory, still more disagreeable was it to certain classes in India to find the man who had already, during his brief sojourn in the East, vehemently assailed the most cherished abuses of Indian misgovernment all at once the victor of a desperate battle. What was to be done in the circumstances? They dared not depreciate the valour of the troops or the desperate bravery they had overcome, but it was possible for them to denounce the victorious old general. He had few friends among the rulers. He had too frequently told them what he thought of them. He had so often applied the salt of his satire to the great leech called favouritism, that now his detractors were sure of finding an audience ready to applaud when they launched the envenomed shaft, and spoke of the "ferocity and blood-thirstiness" of the old chief, and did what they could to lessen his glory,—that chief who wrote in his journal how he had covered an enemy who had come too close to him with his pistol, "but did not shoot, having great repugnance to kill with my own hand unless attacked!"

It is a sorry story, and one we will gladly pass on from with this observation. It would have been better had Napier treated the whole host of his attackers, Indian editors and Indian civilians, English peers and English pressmen, with silent contempt. The very virulence of their denunciation was as quicksilver poured upon the glass of their envy. He could see his own greatness all the better, and measure the shallowness of the medium that revealed it to him. But there was one thing that the detractors could not do; they could not hide from the soldiers of England or India, or from the people of the United Kingdom, that this battle of Meanee had been a victory with the old ring in it. Right up comes the little army; no hesitation, no false movements; right thrown forward because the Irish are there; left thrown back because the enemy's guns are there; then a hand-to-hand fight for three hours in which the old leader is ever out in front waving his hat, cheering with his shrill voice, getting his hair singed with the closeness of guns going off under his nose. No, they cannot blacken that picture, for every man in the little army has seen it during these three hours, and under its influence the very camp-followers have become daring soldiers. "I bring to your notice," writes the officer commanding the artillery, "the names of three native gun-lascars, who displayed the greatest bravery in dragging the guns up to the edge of the bank, level with the Twenty-Second line. I would not venture to do so had they not been mere followers, entitled to no pension to themselves or reward to their families had they fallen." Such is the force of a general's example.

Before night closed on the field the fruits of the victory were apparent. Six Ameers of Scinde came in and surrendered themselves prisoners of war, bringing with them the keys of Hyderabad, whose tall towers were visible against the horizon five miles to the south. Then Napier lay down to sleep, and so sound was his rest that when there is a false alarm among the camp-followers towards morning they cannot rouse him. Next morning he writes his despatches and tells the story of the fight in short and vivid language. He does not forget the man in the ranks, and for the first time in the history of our wars the private soldier is personally named for his bravery. What a levelling general this is! Yesterday he was levelling his enemies; now to-day he is levelling his friends. They will not like it at home, he thinks.

Well, he cannot help that; they will have to like it some day, and the sooner they begin to learn the better, so off goes the names of Drummer Martin Delaney, and full Private James O'Neill, and Havildar Thackoor Ram, and Subadar Eman Beet, and Trooper Mootee Sing, and many others.

Having buried his dead, rested his living, and sent off his despatches, Napier moved his little army to Hyderabad, hoisted the British flag on the great tower of the fortress, and put his force in camp four miles farther west on the Indus. He was still far from the end of hostilities. He had defeated over thirty thousand Beloochees at Meanee, but there were fifteen thousand more who had not reached the field of battle that day, and these now formed a rallying-point for the bands which had withdrawn from that stubborn fight beaten but not routed. Shere Mahomet, Ameer of Meerpoor, the leader of this force—the only real fighting man among the Scindian princes—had still to be reckoned with, and that reckoning was in no degree rendered easier by the fact that since Meanee, the real weakness of the British in numbers had become known to the whole world of Scinde. Everybody had seen the slender column that had taken possession of Hyderabad, and was now entrenched on the left bank of the Indus four miles from the city. Let the Lion of Meerpoor bide his time, gather all the Beloochee clansmen, and when the sun once more hung straight over the Scindian desert fall on the Feringhee. It was a pretty plan, and no doubt might have had fair chance of at least a temporary success had it been played against a less experienced enemy than this old war-dog now entrenched upon the Indus. For him two things were necessary. First, he must obtain reinforcements for his army; second, he must draw the Lion closer to his camp. When the time comes for making another spring it will not do to go seeking this Scindian chief afar off, in deserts that are glowing like live coals in the midsummer sun. So two lines of policy are pursued by Napier. He sends up and down the Indus for every man and gun he hopes to lay hands on, and he spreads abroad in Hyderabad the story of his own weakness. The Lion, scared by Meanee, had fallen back towards his deserts; now, lured by these accounts of paucity of numbers, sickness, etc., he draws forward again, until he is only six miles beyond Hyderabad and within one march of the Indus. It was now the middle of March; the reinforcements are approaching. Stack with fifteen hundred men and five guns is only five marches distant to the north. The Lion can strike at Stack before he joins Napier, but on his side Sir Charles is watchful. If the Lion moves to fall on Stack, he, Napier, will make a spring at the Lion's flank. It is a pretty game, but one of course only possible to play in war with a half-savage enemy. On March 22nd Stack is passing Meanee. The Lion makes a weak attempt to gobble up his fifteen hundred men, but Napier has sent out a strong force of cavalry and guns to help his lieutenant, and Stack gets safely in on the 22nd. On the same day boats arrive from north and south with more reinforcements and supplies, and on the following everything is ready for the attack on the Lion, who is just nine miles distant, entrenched up to his eyes and tail in woods, *nullahs*, and villages at Dubba, five miles from Hyderabad.

Napier has five thousand men all told, the Lion has five-and-twenty thousand. The odds are long, but longer ones had been faced at Meanee, and the Tipperary men are still at the head of the column, and neither they nor their general have the slightest doubt about the result. The army marches before daybreak, and the morning is yet young when it is in sight of the enemy. The Lion is lying low, well hidden in his *nullahs* of which he has a double line, one flank resting on the village of Dubba and the old Fullalee channel, the other well screened by wood. He has eleven guns in front of Dubba. The British column now forms line as at Meanee, but this time the Twenty-Second take the left, opposite the fortified village and the battery, because there will be the thick of the fight. The advance is again to be in *échelon* of battalions, the Twenty-Second leading. When all is ready, the guns, of which Napier has nineteen, open on the Beloochee position, then the Twenty-Second lead straight upon Dubba. Into the *nullah*, through the *nullah*, out of the *nullah*, right through the double line of entrenchments goes this "ever-glorious regiment," strewing the ground with enemies, and leaving more than a third of its own numbers down too. The fighting here and at the village of Dubba is very stubborn, for at this point the brave African chief Hoche Mahomet has taken his stand, and the fierce valour— which forty years later we are to know more about—marks his presence. But Meanee has taken the steel out of the Beloochee swordsmen, and the whole position is soon in our hands. This time Napier is strong in cavalry, and a vigorous pursuit followed the broken bands as they retreated towards Meerpoor. In this fight at Dubba as at Meanee Napier has many escapes. A bullet breaks the hilt of his sword; the orderly riding behind him has his horse disabled with a sword-cut; as they gain the village a magazine blows up in the midst of them; but the General is not touched. As usual he is in the very thick of the fighting, cheered everywhere by the soldiers. They are all young enough to be his children, but they watch him as a lioness would watch her last remaining cub, Private Tim Kelly constituting himself as special protector, and bayoneting every Beloochee that comes near his child. Six months later we find Napier has not forgotten these splendid soldiers. Writing to the Governor-General and thanking him for the promise of a medal for the battles, he thus speaks of his men: "Now I can wear my Grand Cross at ease, but while my officers and men received nothing my Ribbon sat uncomfortably on my shoulder. Now I can meet Corporal Tim Kelly and Delaney the bugler without a blush." And then comes a bit which deserves record so long as history tells of heroism. Here it is: "I find that twelve wounded men of the Twenty-Second concealed their wounds at Dubba, thinking there would be another fight. They were discovered by a long hot march which they could not complete, and when they fell they had to own the truth. Two of them had been shot clean through both legs. How is it possible to defeat British troops? It was for the Duke of York to discover that!"

From the field of Dubba the victors pressed on to finish the war. Two days after the fight the infantry are twenty, and the cavalry forty, miles from the scene of battle. The Lion's capital, Meerpoor, was occupied on March 26th, his desert fort at Omercote surrendered on April 4th. The war was practically over. "This completes the conquest of Scinde," writes Napier when he hears that Omercote is his; "every place is in my possession, and, thank God, I have done with war! Never again am I likely to see another shot fired in anger. Now I shall work at Scinde as in Cephalonia to do good, to create, to improve, to end destruction, to raise up order." So he hoped; but it was not to be as he thought. Peace was yet some months distant, and even when it came with Beloochee on the Indus, a warfare of words and pens with a whole host of enemies at home and in India was to embitter the remaining future of the conqueror's life. The Lion got clear away from Dubba, and by the middle of May he had again rallied to his standard some ten thousand men. He was now fifty miles north of Hyderabad, on the line Napier had followed when moving from Sukkur to Meanee. The heat was at its worst. No one who has not felt the power of the sun in lands where the desert acts as a vast fire-brick to scorch life to a cinder can realise this terrible temperature. One only chance remains for European life under such conditions—it is entire abstinence from alcoholic drink. In Scinde as in other parts of India alcohol was plentiful, and the loss among the soldiers was proportionally great. In the end of May Napier moved once more against the Lion. Two other columns were also directed from north and east against him. Thus between the three advancing forces and the Indus it was hoped he might be crushed. Despite terrific heat and an inundation now at its height, these columns gradually drew to their object; but there was no real fight now left in the Beloochee clansmen; Roberts near Schwan, and Jacob at Shadadpoor, defeated his soldiers with ease, and the Lion became a fugitive in the foot-hills of Beloochistan. It was full time for hostilities to cease. On June 14th Napier's column reached Nusserpoor, some ten or twelve miles east of Meanee; his men were dropping by scores; the air seemed to be on fire. Suddenly through this furnace-heated atmosphere came the distant sound of cannon. It was the last echo of the war; Jacob was fighting the Lion twenty miles to the north. When mid-day arrived the heat grew more intense. In one hour forty-three European soldiers were down with sunstroke, and before evening they were all dead. One more had to fall before the terrible day was over. It was the General. He was sitting writing in his tent, and had just written: "Our lives are on the *simmer* now, and will soon boil; the natives cannot stand it; and I have been obliged to take my poor horse, Red Rover, into my tent, where he lies down exhausted, and makes me very hot. I did not bring a thermometer—what use would it be to lobster boiling alive?" Then he fell struck by heat apoplexy. Fortunately the doctors were near, all the restoratives were quickly applied, and life was saved. As they were tying up his arm after bleeding, a horseman came galloping to the tent. He carried a despatch from Jacob announcing the final victory over Shere Mahomet. What effect the news had on the prostrate old soldier we learn from the journal ten days later, when he is able again to write an entry. "Jacob's message roused me from my lethargy as much as the bleeding; it relieved my mind, for then I knew my plans had succeeded, and the Beloochee had found that his deserts and his fierce sun could not stop me. We lost many men by heat; but all must die some time, and no time better than when giving an enemy a lesson."

They brought him back to Hyderabad, and the wonderful constitution, tempered and twisted into birdcage wire by years of temperance and labour, again asserted itself, and within a fortnight of the blow of the sun he comes up smiling to the hundred cares of war and government, and to the still more wearing worries of assault from open and concealed enemies in England and India. For a long time he is very weak. All the reaction of these four anxious months, all the waste of life-power which war brings with it, now capped by sunstroke, and still further accentuated by calumny and ill-natured criticism, are too much for him, and it seems that he must soon lay his bones in the sands of Scinde. "Even to mount my horse," he writes, "is an exertion. I, who ten years ago did not know what fatigue was, and who even a few months ago at Poonah knocked off fifty-four miles in the heat, am now distressed by four miles! This last illness has floored me, and even my mind has lost its energy; yet it is good to die in harness." These forebodings were not to be verified. The long Scindian summer wore away, and with the end of August cooler weather began to dawn on the Unhappy Valley. Gradually we find the old tone coming back into the journal, the old ring into the letters. He has a hundred plans for the improvement of Scinde and the happiness of its people. He will chain the Indus in its channel, cut canals for irrigation, lessen the taxes, lighten the lot of the labourer, curb the power of the chiefs—in fine, make a Happy Valley out of this long dreary, dusty, sun-baked land. Alas! it was only a pleasant dream. The man who would do all this must be something more than a governor reporting home by every mail, and called upon to reply to every silly question which ignorance, prompted by mammon or malice, may dictate. One thing he is determined upon. He will give the labourer justice, cost what it may. He has caught two tax-collectors riding roughshod over the peasants. "I will make," he writes, "such an example of them as shall show the poor people my resolution to protect them. Yes, I will make this land happy if life is left me for a year. I shall have no more Beloochees to kill. Battle! victory! spirit-stirring sounds in the bosom of society; but to me—O God, how my spirit rejects them! Not one feeling of joy or exultation entered my head at Meanee or Dubba—all was agony. I can use no better word. To win was the least bloody thing to be done, and was my work for the day; but with it came anxiety, pain of heart, disgust, and a longing never to have quitted Celbridge; to have passed my life in the 'round field,' and in the 'devil's acre,' and under the yew trees on the terrace amongst the sparrows—these were the feelings that flashed in my head after the battles." And then he goes on to speak his thoughts upon government and justice, and very noticeable thoughts they are too—never more worthy of attention than to-day. "People think," he writes, "and justly sometimes, that to execute the law is the great thing; they fancy this to be *justice*. Cast away details, good man, and take what the people call justice, not what the laws call justice, and execute that. Both legal and popular justice have their evils, but assuredly the people's justice is a thousand times nearer to God's justice. Justice must go with the people, not against the people; that is the way to govern nations, and not by square and compass." Very old words these, rung so often in the ears of rulers that they have long ago forgotten their import, until all at once their truth is brought home to heart again by the loss of a crown or the revolt of a colony.

Now arrived from England the list of honours and rewards for the victories. Immediately upon the receipt of the news of Meanee Lord Ellenborough had appointed Napier Governor of Scinde, with fullest powers. The *Gazette* made him only a Grand Cross of the Bath. Peerages had been bestowed for very small fractions of victory in Afghanistan; but for these real triumphs in Scinde there was to be no such reward, and it was better that it should have been so. The gold of Napier's nature did not want the stamp of mere rank; perhaps it would not carry the alloy which the modern mint finds necessary for the operation. But although the reward of the victor was thus carefully limited, it was quite sufficient to call forth many open expressions of ill-will, and still more numerous secret assaults of envious antagonists. Unfortunately for Napier, these he could not meet with silent contempt. The noble nature of the man could accept neglect with stoical indifference; but the fighting nature of the soldier could not brook the stings of political or journalistic cavillers. And it must be acknowledged these last were enough to rouse the lion of St. Mark himself, even had that celebrated animal imbibed from his master his full share of virtues. Everything was cavilled at; motive, action, and result were attacked, and from the highest Director of the East India Company in Leadenhall Street to the most insignificant editor of an Indian newspaper in the service of the civilian interest in Bombay or Calcutta, came the stinging flight of query, innuendo, or direct condemnation. The reason for much of this animosity was not hard to find. Napier had dared to tell unpalatable truths about the impoverishment of India through the horde of locusts who, under the name of Government, had settled upon it. The man who could tell the Directors of the East India Company that their military policy tended to the mutiny of their soldiers, and their civil system was a huge source of Indian spoliation, was not likely to find much favour with the richest and most powerful, and, it may be added, the most commercial company the world has ever seen; nor was he likely to be a *persona grata* with the officials who administered the affairs of that gigantic corporation. This is the true key to solve the now perplexing question of the antagonism encountered by Charles Napier from the moment of his success at Meanee to the end of his life. The pride of aristocratic privilege in high place is a dangerous thing to touch; but the pride of the plutocratic Solomon in his right to reap the labour of those who toil and spin is a thousand times a more venturesome thing to trench upon. Added to these causes for negative recognition of brilliant service, and positive condemnation from many quarters, there was a political state of things which influenced the opinion of the moment. Lord Ellenborough was not popular. The Whig policy of action beyond the Indian frontier had been most disastrous. The contrast between it and the campaign on the Indus was painfully apparent. It was like some long day of storm and gloom which had closed in a glorious sunset; and while the morning and mid-day of tempest had been Whig, the evening glory had come under a Tory administration. In reading the history of all these squabbles now, the chief regret we experience is that Napier should have bothered himself with their presence. Indeed, in his moments of calm reflection he appears to have rated them at their true worth. "Honours!" he writes about this time; "I have had honour sufficient in both battles. At Meanee, when we forced the Fullalee, the Twenty-Second, seeing me at their head, gave me three cheers louder than all the firing. And at Dubba, when I returned nearly alone from the pursuit with the cavalry, the whole Line gave me three cheers. One wants nothing more than the praise of men who know how to judge movements."

With these soldiers indeed, officers and men, his popularity was unbounded. They knew the truth. Many among them had seen to their cost the fruits of bad leadership in Cabul, and had learnt to value the truth of the old Greek proverb, which declared that "a herd of deer led by a lion was more formidable to the enemy than a herd of lions led by a deer." And they knew that though this small, spare, eagle-beaked and falcon-eyed leader worked them till they dropped beneath the fierce sun of Scinde, there was no heat of sun or fatigue of march or press of battle which he did not take his lion's share of. Even when now, in this autumn of 1843, an enemy more formidable to soldiers attacked them, when the deadliest fever stalked through the rough camps along the Indus, and the graveyards grew as the ranks thinned, no murmur rose from the rank and file, but silently the fate was accepted which sent hundreds of them to an inglorious death. Here and there through the journals we come on entries that tell more powerfully than any record of figures could do what this mortality must have been. "Alas!" we read only a few months after Meanee, "these two brave soldiers, Kelly and Delaney of the Twenty-Second, are dead. They fought by my side, Kelly at Dubba and Delaney at Meanee. Three times, when I thought the Twenty-Second could not stand the furious rush of the swordsmen, Delaney sounded the advance, and each time the line made a pace or two nearer to the enemy." Difficult now is it for us to believe that at this time, when the soldiers of the army of Scinde were dying by hundreds in hospital, they were denied the last consolations of their religion. "There is no Catholic clergyman here," writes Napier in October, 1843. "The Mussulman and the Hindoo have their teachers; the Christian has none. The Catholic clergyman is more required than the Protestant, because Catholics are more dependent upon their clergy for religious consolation than the Protestants are; and the Catholic soldier dies in great distress if he has not a clergyman to administer to him. But, exclusive of all other reasons, I can hardly believe that a Christian government will refuse his pastor to the soldier serving in a climate where death is so rife, and the buoyant spirit of man is crushed by the debilitating effects of disease and heat. I cannot believe that such a government will allow Mammon to cross the path of our Saviour, to stand between the soldier and his God, and let his drooping mind thirst in vain for the support which his Church ought to afford." No wonder that the Governor who could, in such glowing words, rebuke the greed of his governors and champion the cause of the lowly should find few friends in high place; that the reward of rank, given before and since for such trivial result or such maculated victory, should have been denied to the brilliant victor of Meanee and conqueror of Scinde; that the thanks of Parliament should have been delayed till the greater part of the army thanked was in its grave; and that the leader of that army should find himself and his victories the objects of all the secret shafts and mysterious machinery which wealth, power, and malevolent envy could set in motion against him.

CHAPTER XI
THE ADMINISTRATION OF SCINDE

Scinde subdued in the open field, there still remained great work to be done—work which tasks to a far larger degree the talent of man than any feat of arms in war can do. War at best is but a pulling down, often a very necessary operation, but all the same only the preliminary step of clearing the ground for some better edifice.

For better, for worse, Scinde was now British, and Napier set at once to work to consolidate his conquest, and secure to the conquered province the best administration of justice he could devise for it. A terrible misfortune came, however, to retard all plans for improvement. Early in the autumn pestilence laid low almost the entire army of the Indus. A slow and wasting form of fever broke out among both English and Indian soldiers, and equally struck down the natives of Scinde. In the camp at Hyderabad twenty-eight hundred men were down together. At Kurachee the Twenty-Eighth Regiment could only muster about forty men fit for service out of the entire battalion. At Sukkur, in Northern Scinde, sixteen hundred were in hospital. There were only a few doctors to look after this army of sick. Out of three cavalry regiments, only a hundred men could mount their horses. People shook their heads gloomily, and Scinde became known far and wide as the Unhappy Valley. Amid all this misery, while "the land in its length and breadth was an hospital," as Napier described it, we find him never giving in for a moment, working at his plans for justice, repression of outrage, irrigation, roads, bridges, moles, harbours, and embankments as though he was enjoying the health-giving breezes of the Cephalonian mountains. Wonderful now to read are the plans and visions of the future that then floated before his mind. "Suez, Bombay, and Kurachee will hit Calcutta hard before twenty years pass," he writes, "but Bombay will beat Kurachee, and be the Liverpool if not the London of India." Nor has the pestilence stilled in his heart dreams of further conquest. "How easily, were I absolute," he says, "could I conquer all these countries and make Kurachee the capital. With the Bombay soldiers of Meanee and Hyderabad I could walk through all the lands. I would raise Beloochee regiments, pass the Bolan in a turban, and spread rumours of a dream and the prophet. Pleasant would be the banks of the Helmund to the host of Mahomedans who would follow any conqueror." So passed the winter of 1844. Before the cool season was over, the troops had regained comparative health, and were better able to face the terrible summer. May and June came, as usual bringing sunstroke, disease, and death in their train, but for Napier the hot season of 1844 had something worse in store. His Chief, Lord Ellenborough, was suddenly recalled by the East India Directors. This was a regular knock-down blow, for while Lord Ellenborough was Viceroy of India Charles Napier could count upon an unvarying support; he fought, as it were, with his back to a wall. Now the wall was gone, and henceforth it seemed that the circle of his enemies would be complete. "I see but one advantage in the unfortunate recall of Lord Ellenborough," he writes; "it will oblige the Government to destroy a Mercantile Republic which has arisen in the midst of the British Monarchy." The prophecy was not to be fulfilled for thirteen years, when the terrible mutiny of 1857—so often predicted by Napier, and laughed at by his enemies—came like an avalanche to sweep before it every vestige of the famous Association.

What life in Scinde meant to Napier in this hot season of 1844 we gather from a letter written in June to his brother. "The Bengal troops at Shikarpoor are in open mutiny," he writes, "and I am covered with boils, that have for three weeks kept me in pain and eight days in bed. This, with the heat and an attack of fever, has made me too weak to go to Shikarpoor, for the sun is fierce up the river; many have been struck down by it last week, and it would be difficult for me to bear a second rap. Still I would risk it, but that a storm seems brewing at Mooltan, and this extraordinary change of governors will not dispel it. To me also it appears doubtful, if the Sikhs pour sixty or seventy thousand men over the Sutlej, whether Gough has means to pull them up. I am therefore nursing myself to be able to bolt northwards when we can act, which is impossible now—three days under canvas would kill half the Europeans." If Napier's reputation for foresight stood alone upon the above letter, it would suffice to place him at the top of the far-seeing leaders of his day. In the midst of all his sickness and discomfort he accurately forecast the history of the coming years in India. The intense activity of the man's mind is never more apparent than during this terrible season, which prostrates thousands of younger men. His letters teem with brilliant bits of thought on government, war, justice, society, politics, taxation,—nothing comes amiss to him. Here, for example, is a bit on war worth whole volumes of the stuff usually written about it. "The man who leads an army cannot succeed unless his whole mind is thrown into his work, any more than an actor can act unless he feels his part as if he was the man he represents. It is not saying 'Come and go' that wins battles; you must make the men you lead come and go with a will to their work of death. The man who either cannot or will not do this, but goes to war snivelling about virtue and unrighteousness, will be left on the field of battle to fight for himself." Here again is a little chapter on Indian government. "The Indian system seems to be the crushing of the native plebeian and supporting the aristocrat who, reason and facts tell us, is our deadly enemy. He always must be, for we step into his place. The *ryot* is ruined by us, though willing to be our friend. Yet he is the man to whom we must trust for keeping India—and the only one who can take it from us, if we ill-use him, for then he joins his hated natural chief. English and Indian may be amalgamated by just and equal laws—until we are no longer strangers. The final result of our Indian conquests no man can predict, but if we take the people by the hand we may count on ruling India for ages. Justice—rigid justice, even severe justice—will work miracles. India is safe if so ruled, but such deeds are done as make me wonder that we hold it a year."

As the cool season of 1844-45 drew on, Napier set out on an expedition against the hill tribes of Northern Scinde. Hitherto these wild clansmen had had things pretty much their own way; in true Highland fashion they were wont to sweep down upon the villages of the plain, killing men, carrying off women and cattle, looting and devastating as they went. Hard to catch were these Beloochee freebooters, for their wiry little horses carried the riders quickly out of reach into some fastness where pursuit, except in strength and with supplies for man and beast, was hopeless. The hills which harboured these raiders ran along the entire western frontier of Scinde, from the sea to the Bolan Pass. North of that famous entrance to Afghanistan they curved to the east, approaching the Indus not far from the point where that stream received the five rivers of the Punjaub. Here, spreading out into a labyrinth of crag, defile, and mountain, they formed a succession of natural fortresses, the approaches to which were unknown to the outer world. This great fastness, known as the Cutchee Hills, was distant from Kurachee more than three hundred miles. Leaving Kurachee in the middle of November and following a road which skirted a fringe of hills lying west of the Indus, Napier reached his northern frontier after a month's march. It was a pleasant change to get away from the sickly cantonments into the desert and the hills, where the pure air, now cooled by the winter nights, brought back health and strength to the little column. How thoroughly the toil- and heat-worn soldier enjoyed this long march we gather from his letters.

> My march is a picturesque one (he writes). At this moment behind me is my Mogul guard, some two hundred cavalry, with their splendid Asiatic dress, and the sun's horizontal rays glancing with coruscations of light along their bright sword-blades. Behind them are three hundred infantry— the old bronzed soldiers of the Thirteenth Regiment—the defenders of Jellalabad, veterans of battle. So are the cavalry, for they charged at Meanee and Hyderabad, where their scarlet turbans were seen sweeping through the smoke—by their colour seeming to announce the bloody

work they were at. On these picturesque horsemen the sun is gleaming, while the Lukkee hills are casting their long shades and the Kurta range reflects from its crowning rock the broad beautiful lights. Below me are hundreds of loaded camels with guards and drivers, rude grotesque people, all slowly winding among the hills. Such is royal life here, for it is grand and kingly to ride through the land that we have conquered, with the men who fought. Yet, what is it all? Were I a real king there would be something in it—but a mere copper captain!

A fine picture of martial life in the East all the same, and when we contrast it with a little bit of his experience a couple of days later, we get the far-apart limits which held between them the nature of the man. He is now writing from Schwan, where he has delayed his march two days for the purpose of seeing justice done to the poor cultivators and fishermen of that place.

November 30th.—Still at Schwan, having halted to find out the truth. The poor people came to me with earnest prayers,—they never come without cause,—but they are such liars and so bad at explaining, that were their language understood by me it would be hard to reach facts. Yet, knowing well that at the bottom there is gospel, that no set of poor wretches ever complain without a foundation, here will I stay until the truth comes out, and relief be given. On all these occasions my plan is a most unjust one, for against all evidence I decide in favour of the poor, and argue against the argument of the Government people as long as I can. When borne down by proofs 'irrefragable,' like Alexander, I cut the knot and give an atrocious verdict against 'clearest proof.' My formula is this: punish the Government servants first, and inquire about the right and wrong when there is time. This is the way to prevent tyranny, to make the people happy, and to render public servants honest. If the complaint is that they cheat Government, oh! that is another question; then have fair trials and leniency. We are all weak when temptation is strong.

Pity is it to lose a word of this ruler, who rules in fashion so different from the law-giving of the usual bigwig. But space denies us longer leave to delve in this rich mine of justice. It is a fine picture—one that the world does not see enough of—this victorious old soldier riding through the conquered land intent on justice, sparing himself nothing to lift up the poor, to free the toiler, to unbind the slave. A strong man, terrible only to the unjust, spreading everywhere the one grand law of his life—"A privileged class cannot be permitted." With him the quibbler, the *doctrinaire*, the political economist, has no place. "Well did Napoleon say," he writes, "that the *doctrinaire* and the political economist would ruin the most flourishing kingdom in ten years. Well, they have no place yet in Scinde; there are no Whig poor-laws here. Oh, it is glorious thus to crush Scindian Whiggism! and don't I grind it till my heart dances? The poor fishermen who are now making their lying howls of complaint at the door of my tent are right, though I can't yet find the truth in the midst of their falsehoods." But he stops by the shore of Lake Manchur until the truth is found out; and then we read: "Marched this morning, having penetrated the mystery. The collector has without my knowledge raised the taxation 40 per cent on the very poorest class of the population. He is an amiable man, and so religious that he would not cough on a Sunday, yet he has done a deed of such cruelty as is enough to raise an insurrection. This discovery of oppression is alone sufficient to repay the trouble of my journey." A despot, you will say, reader, is this soldier judge, thus

Riding forth redressing human wrong.

Yes, a despot truly, and one who, if history had held more of them, we might to-day have known a good deal less about human misery than we do. And now with your permission we will proceed into the Cutchee Hills.

Napier reached Sukkur in the week preceding Christmas 1844. It had been the base from whence he had moved to attack the Ameers two years earlier. It was now to be his base against the hill tribes of Cutchee. At the head of a confederacy of clans stood Beja Khan Doomkee, an old and redoubtable warrior, strong in the inaccessible nature of his mountains, strong, too, in being able to throw the glamour of Islam over his raids and ravages, and stronger still in the bravery and determination of the men whose creed of plunder was strangely coupled with the old heroic virtues of that great Arab race from which they sprang. How was this stout old robber with his eight or ten thousand fighting men to be worsted? By the exact opposite of the ordinary rules of war for civilised opponents: by dispersing the columns of attack, while making each strong enough for separate resistance, he would force the clansmen to mass together; the very ruggedness and aridity which made their hills so formidable to an enemy would thus be turned against themselves. Napier's columns, fed from their bases on the Indus, would advance cautiously into the labyrinth; the hill-men, forced together in masses, would eat out their supplies; the same walls of rock which kept out an enemy would now keep in the assembled tribes.

Before setting his columns in motion from the Indus, Napier adopted many devices to lull the clans into a fancied security. The fever still clung to his soldiers, and so deadly was its nature that nearly the whole of the Seventy-Eighth Highlanders perished at Sukkur. But even this terrible disaster was turned to account by the inexhaustible resource of the commander. He sent messages to the Khan of Khelat that the sickness of his soldiers and his own debility were so great that he could not move against the tribes. These messages were designed to reach Beja Khan. They did reach him, and emboldened by the news the hill-men remained with their flocks and herds on the level and comparatively fertile country where the desert first merges into the foot-hills of Cutchee. Then Napier, suddenly launching his force in three columns, dashed into this borderland by forced marches, surprised the tribes, captured thousands of their cattle and most of their grain supplies, and forcing them back into the mountains, sat down himself at the gates or passes leading into the fastness to await the arrival of his guns, infantry, and commissariat. It took some days before his columns were ready to enter the defiles, and then the real mountain warfare began. Very strange work it was; full of necessities of sudden change, of ceaseless activity, of prolonged exertion, climbing of rocks, boring for water, meeting each day's difficulty by some fresh combination, some new expedient. A war where set rules did not apply, where the savage had to be encountered by equal instinct and wider comprehension, but where, nevertheless, the sharpest foresight was as essential to success as though the theatre of the struggle had been on the soldier-trodden plains of Europe. Broadly speaking, the plan of campaign was this. He would enter the hills with four columns, one of which, his own, would be the real fighting one; the other three would act as stoppers of the main passes leading out of the mountains. Somewhere in the centre of the cluster of fastnesses there was a kernel fastness called Truckee. It was a famous spot in the robber legends of middle Asia, a kind of circular basin having a wall of perpendicular rock six hundred feet high all round it, with cleft entrance only at two places, one opening north, the other south. The object of Napier's strategy was to compel the hill-men to enter this central stronghold, for if once there, they were at his mercy. But before he could force them into this final refuge he had to learn for himself the paths and passes of the entire region, finding out where there was water, securing each pass behind him before he made a step forward in advance.

It was early January when the advance began. March had come before the last move was played on the rugged chessboard, and Beja Khan and his men were safe in Truckee. During all that interval the Commander's spirit never seems to have flagged for a moment. Scattered through his journal we find many instances of his having to find mental spirits for his followers as well as for himself. There had been numerous prophecies of failure from many quarters. "It was a wild-goose chase"—"Beja Khan was too old and wary a bird to be caught"—"Beware of the mountain passes,"—so ran the chorus of foreboding; and whenever a check occurred or a delay had to be made for supplies, from these prophets of disaster could be heard the inevitable "I told you so." That terrible croak in war which half tells that the wish to retire is at least stepfather to the thought of failure. Here is a little journal-picture which has a good deal of future history in it. "*February 6th.*—Waiting for provisions; this delay is bad. Simpson is in the dismals, so am I, but that won't feed us." Simpson belonged to that large class of excellent officers who just want one thing to be good chiefs. Ten and a half years later Simpson, still in the dismals, sat looking at his men falling back, baffled, from the Russian Redan at Sebastopol. Perhaps had Napier been there he would have been baffled too. It may be so, but in that case I think they would have had to seek him under the muzzles of the Russian guns.

Scared by the passes through which the convoys had to move, the camel-drivers had deserted with five hundred camels, leaving the column without food; but Napier was equal to the emergency. Dismounting half his fighting camel-corps he turned that Goliah of war, Fitzgerald, into a commissariat man for the moment, sent him back for flour, and six days later has forty-four thousand pounds of bread-stuff in his camp. How terribly anxious are these moments when a commander finds himself and his troops at the end of his food-tether no one but a commander of troops can ever know. It is such moments that lay bare the bed-rock of human nature, and show at once what stuff it is made of—granite, or mere sandstone that the rush of events will wash away in the twinkling of an eye. What stuff formed this bed-rock of Charles Napier's nature one anecdote will suffice to show. During the two years that he has now been at war in Scinde, fighting foes and so-called friends, fighting disease, sun, distance, old age, and bodily weakness, he has never ceased to send to his two girls left behind at Poonah, in Bombay, quires of foolscap paper with sums in arithmetic, questions in grammar, and lessons in geography duly set out for answer. While he is Governor and Commander-in-Chief of Scinde he is acting governess to his children fifteen hundred miles away in Bombay. The only other instance of similar mental power that I know of is to be found in the directions for the internal improvement of France, and the embellishment of her towns and cities, sent by Napoleon from the snowy bivouacs of the Baltic provinces and the slaughters of Heilsbronn and Eylau. Of course it was to be expected that the desertion of the camel-transport, and the attacks of the robbers upon the line of communications which preceded the flight of the camel-men, should have increased to a dangerous extent the forebodings of failure. Napier is furious. "I am fairly put to my trumps by this desertion," he writes. "Well, exertion must augment. I will use the camel-corps, and dismount half my cavalry, if need be. I will eat my horse,

Red Rover, sooner than flinch before these robber tribes. My people murmur, but they only make my foot go deeper into the ground."

How lightly the eye scans such passages, and yet beneath them lies the whole secret of success in war. "How easy then it must be," I think I hear some reader say. "You have only to stick your heels in the sand, cry out, 'I won't go back,' and the game is yours." Not so fast, good friend. Blondin's crossing the chasm of Niagara was very easy to Blondin, but woe betide the other man who ventured to try it. There were generals even in our own time who thought they could copy Napier's method of war, but what a terrible mess they made of it! The thing is indeed very easy when you know how to do it, but that little secret is only to be learned through long years of study and experience, and even then it is only to be mastered by a select few. Make no mistake about it, good reader. History is right when she walks behind great soldiers noting their deeds. They are the rarest human products which she meets with.

When Beja Khan and his confederate sirdars found themselves shut up within the walls of Truckee they gave up the game and asked permission to surrender. Leave was granted, and on March 9th they came out and laid their swords at Napier's feet. With all their love of plunder they were very splendid warriors, these Doomkee, Bhoogtee, and Jackranee chiefs and clansmen, holding notions of the honour of arms which more civilised soldiers would do well to follow. Here is one such notion. When Charles Napier stood before the southern cleft or pass which gave entrance to Truckee, another column under Beatson blocked the northern gate of the stronghold. Although the two passes were only distant from each other in a straight line across the labyrinth some half-dozen miles, they were one or more days' journey asunder by the circuitous road round the flank of the mountain rampart. One column therefore knew nothing of the other's proceedings. While waiting thus opposite the northern entrance Beatson determined to reconnoitre the interior of the vast chasm by scaling the exterior wall of rock. For this purpose a part of the old Thirteenth, veterans of Jellalabad, was sent up the mountain; the ascent, long and arduous, was all but completed when it was observed from below that the flat top of the rock held a strong force of the enemy, entrenched behind a breastwork of stones. The ascending body of the Thirteenth numbered only sixteen men, the enemy on the summit was over sixty. In vain the officer who made this discovery tried to warn the climbers of the dangers so close above them, but which they could not see; his signs were mistaken by the men for fresh incentives to advance, and they pushed on towards the top instead of retracing their steps to the bottom. As the small party of eleven men gained the summit they were greeted by a matchlock volley from the low breastwork in front, followed by the charge of some seventy Beloochees, sword in hand. The odds were desperate; the Thirteenth men were blown by the steep ascent; the ground on which they stood was a dizzy ledge, faced by the stone breastwork and flanked by tremendous precipices. No man flinched; fighting with desperate valour they fell on that terrible but glorious stage, in sight of their comrades below, who were unable to give them help. Six out of the eleven fell at once; five others, four of them wounded, were pushed over the rocks, rolling down upon their half-dozen comrades who had not yet gained the summit. How hard they fought and died one incident will tell. Private John Maloney, fighting amid a press of enemies, and seeing two comrades, Burke and Rohan, down in the *melée*, discharged two muskets into the breast of a Beloochee, and ran another through with his bayonet. The Beloochee had strength and courage to unfix the bayonet, draw it from his body, and stab Maloney with his own weapon before he himself fell dead upon the rock. Maloney, although severely wounded, made good his retreat and brought off his two comrades. So much for the fighting on both sides. Now for the chivalry of those hill-men. When a chief fell bravely in battle it was an old custom among the clans to tie a red or green thread around his right or left wrist, the red thread on the right wrist being the mark of highest valour. Well, when that evening the bodies of the six slain soldiers were found at the foot of the rocks, rolled over from the top by the Beloochee garrison above, each body had a red thread, not on one wrist, but on both.[4]

The expedition against the hill tribes was over, but larger warfare was at hand. North of Scinde a vast region of unrest lay simmering in strife. Runjeet Singh was dead, and the great army he had called into being was rapidly pushing the country to the brink of the precipice of war. Napier had long predicted the Punjaub war, but his warnings had been lightly listened to, and when in December, 1846, the Sikhs suddenly threw a large force across the Sutlej, they found a British army cantoned far in front of its magazines, unprovided with the essentials of a campaign—reserve ammunition and transport—able to fight, indeed, with all the vehemence of its old traditions, but lacking that leadership which, by power of forecast and preparation, draws from the courage of the soldier the utmost result of victory.

Between December, 1846, and February, 1847, four sanguinary actions were fought on the banks of the Sutlej—the Sikh soldiery were brave and devoted warriors, but of their leaders the most influential were large recipients of English gold, and the remainder were ignorant of all the rules of war. Nevertheless the bravery of the common soldiers made the campaign more than once doubtful, and it was only in the final conflict at Sobraon on February 10th, 1847, that the campaign was decided.

Meanwhile, the steps which Napier had long foreseen as necessary in Scinde, but in the timely execution of which he had been constantly thwarted by higher authority, were ordered to be taken with all despatch. Moodkee and Ferozeshah had suddenly revealed the strength of the Sikh army, and Scinde was looked to in the hour of anxiety for aid against this powerful enemy. With what extraordinary rapidity Napier assembled his army at Roree for a forward movement towards the Punjaub has long passed from the recollection of men. On December 24th the order reached him at Kurachee. Forty-two days later, a most compact fighting force of fifteen thousand men, fifty-four field guns, and a siege-train stood ready, the whole complete for a six months' campaign; so complete indeed in power of movement, capacity for sustained effort, and full possession of all the requisites of war that it might, as an offensive force, be reckoned at twice its actual numbers. Organisation, transport system, and equipment are the wheels of war—without them the best army is but a muzzled bulldog tied to a short chain.

But this admirable force was not to be used. The battle of Sobraon was the prelude to a patched-up peace, which divided the Sikh State, depleted the Sikh treasury, but left intact the Sikh army. The generalship on the Sutlej had been indifferent; the policy that followed the campaign was still larger marked by want of foresight. Napier, ordered to leave his army at Bahawalpore, had proceeded alone to Lahore to advise and assist the negotiations for peace. He joined Hardinge, Gough, and Smith in the Sikh capital, receiving a tremendous ovation from the troops and a cordial welcome from the three chiefs, who, if they were not brilliant generals, were chivalrous and gallant soldiers. It must have been a fine sight these four old warriors of the Peninsula going in state to the palace of the Maharajah at Lahore. Napier, though keen to catch the errors of the campaign, has nothing but honour and regard for his brother-generals. "Gough is a glorious old fellow," he writes; "brave as *ten* lions, each with two sets of teeth and two tails." "Harry Smith did his work well." And of Hardinge's answer to those who urged him to retreat during the night after the first day's carnage at Ferozeshah—"No, we will abide the break of day, and then either sweep all before us or die honourably"—he cannot say too much; but all this does not blind him to the waste of human life that want of foresight had caused. "We have beaten the Sikhs in every action," he writes, "with our glorious, most glorious soldiers, but thousands of those brave men have bit the dust who ought now to be standing sword in hand victorious at the gates of Lahore." "Do you recollect saying to me," he asks his brother, "'Our soldiers will fight any general through his blunders'? Well, now, judge your own prophecy." Finally, all the foresight of the man's mind comes out in these prophetic words, written when the war had just closed, "This tragedy must be reacted a year or two hence; we shall have another war." Chillianwallah and Goojerat had yet to be.

Back to Scinde again to take up the old labour of civil administration, and work out to practical solution a hundred problems of justice, commerce, land-tenure, agriculture, and taxation,—in fine, to build upon the space cleared by war the stately edifice of a wise and beneficent human government, keeping always in view certain fundamental rules of honesty, truth, justice, and wisdom, learned long years before in Ireland at his father's side.

Napier's system of rule was after all a very old one. It went back before ever a political economist set pen to paper. Anybody who will turn to the pages of Massinger will find it set forth clearly enough at the time King and Parliament were coming to loggerheads over certain things called Prerogative and Privilege—words which, if the weal of the soil-tiller be forgotten, are only empty and meaningless balderdash. Here are the men whose goods are lawful prize in the philosophy of the old dramatist—

The cormorant that lives in expectation

Of a long wished-for dearth, and smiling grinds

The faces of the poor;

The grand encloser of the Commons for

His private profit or delight;

      The usurer,

Greedy at his own price to make a purchase,

Taking advantage upon bond or mortgage

From a prodigal—

  These you may grind to powder.

And now these are they who should be spared and shielded:

      The scholar,

Whose wealth lies in their heads and not their pockets;

Soldiers that have bled in their country's service;

The rent-rack'd farmer, needy market-folk;

The sweaty labourer, carriers that transport

The goods of other men—are privileged;

But above all let none presume to offer

Violence to women, for our king hath sworn

Who that way's a delinquent, without mercy

Swings for it, by martial law.

Here we have the pith and essence of Napier's government in Scinde, very simple, and probably containing more law-giving wisdom than half the black-lettered statutes made and provided since Massinger wrote them down two hundred and fifty years ago.

For eighteen months longer—until September, 1847—Napier remained in Scinde, labouring to rule its people on the strictest lines of honest justice. Two more hot seasons scorched his now age-weakened frame, and again came terrible visitations of cholera and fever, to lay low many a gallant friend and make aching gaps in his own domestic circle; but these trials he accepted as a soldier accepts on the battle-field the bullets which whistle as they go,—for want of life. But there was one thing which he could not accept with the same courageous calmness: it was the systematic censure upon his actions, vilification of his motives, and abuse of himself, which deepened in intensity as the load of life grew heavier through age. When a traveller through tropical forests touches a hornets' nest the enraged insects rush out and sting him on the moment; but the hornets' nest which Napier had disturbed in India was not to be appeased by any sudden ebullition of its wrath. Much more slow and deadly was its method. He had dared to speak the honest truth that was in him about the greed and rapacity of London Directors, and the waste, the extravagance, and the luxury of their English servants in the East; he had committed that sin which power never pardons, the championing of the poor and oppressed against the rich and ruling ones of the earth. Now he had to pay the penalty, and from a thousand sources it was demanded at his hands. There was to be no mercy for this man who had not only dared to condemn the abuses of power, but had added the insult of smiting his opponents with the keen Damascus blade of his genius. To condemn plutocratic power has ever been bad enough, but to ridicule the truffle-fed and the truculent tyrant has been a thousand times worse. So for the closing years of his rule in Scinde, and indeed, one may say, almost up to the hour of his death, Napier had to bear slings and arrows that rained upon him from open and from unseen enemies. When the critic of to-day, scanning the pages of the now forgotten literature which deals with this long vituperative contest— sometimes carried on in Parliament, sometimes in the Press, often in books, official papers, and Minutes of Council—he cannot repress a feeling of regret that Napier should ever have noticed a tithe of the abuse and censure which was heaped upon him. Still we must remember that first of all he was a soldier, quick to strike when struck, never counting the cost of his blow against wrong or injustice or oppression of the poor; ever ready to turn his defence into assault, and to storm with brightest and keenest sword-blade the entrenchments of his assailants. One can picture, for instance, the dull rage of some of his ministerial antagonists in this year 1847, when after they had worried him with a thousand queries upon a variety of false accusations circulated by his enemies in Bombay as to his injurious treatment of the cultivators in Scinde, he takes particular pains to inform the Government in England that he can send them eleven thousand tons of wheat from the Indus to feed the then starving people of Ireland. Clearly this was an offence beyond pardon!

In October, 1847, Charles Napier quitted Scinde and set his face for England. He came back broken in health but absolutely unbent in spirit. How full he is of great thoughts—of conquests which should benefit humanity; of freedom which would strike down monopoly and privilege and tyranny; of reform which would not stop short until it had reached the lowest depths of the social system. "Were I Emperor of the East and thirty years of age," he writes, "I would have Constantinople on one side and Pekin on the other before twenty years, and all between should be grand, free, and happy. The Emperor of Russia should be done; freedom and the Press should burn along his frontier like touch-paper until half his subjects were mine in heart." Then he turns to Ireland. To be dictator of that country "would be worth living for." The heads of his system of rule are worth recalling to-day, though they are more than forty years old. First of all he would send "the whole of the bishops and deacons of the Church as by law established to New Zealand, there to eat or to be eaten by cannibals." Then the tillers of the soil should be made secure, a wise system of agriculture taught and enforced, all uncultivated land taxed; then he would hang the editors of noisy newspapers, fire on the mob if it rose against him, and hang its leaders, particularly if they were Catholic priests. But it is very worthy of remark that his drastic measures would not be taken until all other efforts at reform had failed. Poor-law commissioners would have to work on the public roads and all clearers of land be summarily hanged without benefit of clergy. Beneath this serio-comic exposition of Irish government one or two facts are very noticeable. The bishops who had revenue without flocks, and the landlords who wished to have flocks instead of tenants, were given highest place in the penal pillory; after them came the Irish priests and people.

In May, 1848, Napier reached England. He had spent the winter in the Mediterranean, as it was feared his health could ill stand the sudden change from Scinde to an English December. But while loitering by the shores of the sunny sea he is not idle; despite illness and bodily pain his mind is busy recalling the past or forecasting the future. The anniversaries of his Scindian battles call forth the remark, "I would rather have finished the roads in Cephalonia than have fought Austerlitz or Waterloo."

Europe, then seething in the fever fit which threw from her system a good deal of the poison placed in it by the Congress of Vienna, is scanned by the veteran soldier with an eye that gleams again with the old fire at the final triumph of those principles of human right which he had in earlier days loved as a man, though compelled to combat as a soldier. Had we not interfered in the affairs of France there would have been no "'48 Revolution," he writes; "Louis Philippe would have been what nature fitted him for—a pedlar."

When he arrived in England an attempt was made by a small but powerful clique to boycott him, but the people broke the barrier of this wretched enmity, and he was soon taken to the great heart of the nation he had served so well. Amid all the addresses, the dinners, and the congratulations, there comes a little touch that tells us the conqueror's heart is still true to the conscript's love. A Radical shoemaker in Bath has written to welcome home the victor. "I am more flattered by Bolwell's letter," replies the veteran, "than by dinners from all the clubs in London." Many natures stand firm under the rain of adversity, for she is an old and withered hag; only the real hero resists the smiles of success, for she comes hiding the thorn under rosy cheeks and laughing lips.

FOOTNOTE:

[4] It should be unnecessary to remind my readers of the fine poem in which Sir Francis Doyle, whose heart always went out to knightly deeds, has commemorated this incident,—*The Red Thread of Honour.*

CHAPTER XII ENGLAND—1848 TO 1849

From May, 1848, to March, 1849, Napier remained in England. During these ten months his life might fitly be described as a mixture of honour and insult—honour from the great mass of his fellow-countrymen, insult at the hands of the Board of Directors of the East India Company, and from more than one Minister of the Crown. While the military clubs in London and corporate bodies throughout England and Ireland were organising banquets in his honour, the Directors were busily at work depreciating his fame as a soldier, and endeavouring to deprive him of the prize-money taken in the Scinde War; and for the same purpose the cause of the ex-Ameers of Scinde was brought forward and championed by the very persons who at this moment were defending and endeavouring to screen the perfidy recently enacted against the Rajah of Sattara in the interests of the East India Directors.

That Charles Napier resented with exceeding warmth these insults upon his honour and attacks upon his fortune is not matter of surprise, at least to those who have watched his career through all its varying vicissitudes, nor were the times such as would have tended to soothe into quieter temper a mind easily set aflame by the sight of suffering and oppression. This summer of 1848 was indeed a painful period. The shadow of an appalling famine was still passing over Ireland; seven hundred and fifty thousand peasants had already perished from starvation, and the ghastly record was being hourly swelled by fresh victims. From across the Atlantic terrible accounts were arriving of the horrors of the "coffin ships," wherein the famine-wasted refugees perished in such numbers and amid such scenes of human suffering that the records of the old middle passage of the slave-ships from Africa were paralleled if not surpassed. Nor did the story of suffering end when the great gate of refuge, the shore of America, was reached, for the deadly famine fever clung to those who reached the land, and the New World saw repeated in the pest-houses at Quebec, Montreal, Boston, New York, the same awful scenes which Defoe had described nearly two hundred years earlier. Small wonder then if Napier's nature should have flared out at such a time. "I see that violence and '*putting down*' is the cry," he writes. "There is but one way of putting down starving men who take arms—killing them; and one way of hindering them from taking up arms, viz. feeding them. The first seems to engross the thoughts of all who wear broadcloth and gorge on turbot, but there seems no great measure in view for removing suffering," and then comes a reflection that has a strange interest for us to-day: "Yet God knows what will happen, for we see great events often turn out the reverse of what human calculations lead us to expect."

When the summer of 1848 was closing, Napier took a house at Cheltenham for the winter, glad to escape from "those effusions of fish and folly," the London dinners. From here he watched as eagerly as though he had been fifty years younger the progress of events in Northern India, where already all his forecasts of renewed strife were being rapidly realised. Mooltan was up, the Sikhs were again in arms, the true nature of the battles on the Sutlej were made apparent; and those hard-bought victories which the East India Directors and their allies, ignorant of every principle of war, had persisted in blazoning to the world as masterpieces of strategy and tactics, were seen to possess, certainly, the maximum of soldier's courage, but by no means that of general's ability. The Punjaub war had in fact to be fought again. Meanwhile the lesser war between Napier and the Directors went briskly on. The more decidedly events in the East justified the acts and opinions of Napier, the more vehement became the secret hostility against him. Secret warfare formed no part of the Napier tactics, and accordingly we find him blazing out in open warfare against his sly and circumspect traducers. Writing in his journal more than a year before this date, he had foreshadowed for himself the line he would adopt against his adversaries. "There is a vile conspiracy against me," he wrote, "but I defy them all, horse, foot, and dragoons. Now, Charles Napier, be calm! give your enemies no advantage over you by loss of self-control; do nothing that they want, and everything to annoy them; keep your post like a rock, till you are ready to go on board for England; and then with your pen, and your pistols too, if necessary, harass them." Here was his plan of campaign, sketched out clearly enough, plenty of fire and steel in it, no concealment. "The Gauls march openly to battle," had written a Roman historian eighteen hundred years earlier. When the Franks crossed the Rhine they came to graft upon the Gaulish nature a still fairer and franker mode of action. Charles Napier could trace his pedigree back to frankest Frank, and whether he fought a Frenchman in Spain, a Beloochee in Scinde, or an East Indian trader in the city of London, his methods of battle were the same.

Before the year '48 closed, great changes and events had taken place over Europe. France had shaken off her old man of the mountain, Italy was giving many premonitory signs of getting rid of the Austrian, that sinister settlement called the Congress of Vienna was everywhere being undone. Even in Ireland the ferment of revolution was causing a spasmodic twitching in that all but lifeless frame, and desperate men, forgetful of the utter ruin which must await their efforts at revolt, were about to add the final misery of war to the already deeply-tasted evils of famine and pestilence.

And now came an episode of the Irish rising which was closely connected with Charles Napier. In September the leaders of the movement were brought to trial in Clonmel. Sir William Napier, who for the past six years had devoted himself to the task of vindicating his brother's character and actions from the aspersions and assaults of his numerous enemies, had in 1832 been the recipient of a letter, written by the private secretary of a Cabinet Minister, of a very strange nature. No other interpretation could have been justly placed upon this communication except that it was an attempt to sound the then Colonel Napier upon the likelihood of his consenting to lead an armed movement of men from Birmingham to London. Wild though such a project may now appear, there can be no doubt that at the time of the great Reform Bill it was by no means looked upon as lying outside the pale of probability. The news that the Duke of Wellington was about to form an anti-reform administration was received by the people of England with a deep feeling of execration, and resistance was openly proposed and advocated. "To run upon the banks for gold, and to pay no taxes to the State, until reform was granted," were only the preliminary steps which the Whig leaders advised the people to adopt; and it was an open secret that Lord John Russell was prepared to go much further in his scheme of resistance to law in the struggle which the violent opposition of the Lords was forcing upon the nation. It was therefore no stretch of Colonel Napier's imagination to see in the strange letter which he received from the Whig Minister's private secretary a scarcely veiled invitation to draw his sword against what was the existing law of the land. Bad though that law most certainly was, and vehemently though he had opposed it by voice and pen and labour of mind and body, William Napier was still the last man in England to pass the boundary which separates moral from physical antagonism. It is alike the misfortune of thrones and of peoples that around the former there will ever crowd those selfish and self-seeking men whose loyalty is only a cover to hide their own greed of power or possession. These people are the real enemies of kings, for they doubly darken the view which the monarch gets of his people and that which the people get of their king. The Napiers had both been near enough to the Throne to know that it lay a long way beyond the self-seeking crowd which surrounded it, and their hatred of that crowd and of its politics did not go an inch beyond the surrounding circle. To draw his sword against the faction which then stood between the people and their right of reform must be to advance against the Crown, which this faction had cunningly contrived to hang as a breastplate upon their bodies. That fact was sufficient for William Napier, and he not only repudiated the suggestion with all the strength of his nature, but he warned his correspondent that if ever the then leaders of reform should become the dominant faction in the State, and should attempt to play upon the people the same selfish game of obstruction or to prosecute others for resorting to similar methods of force, he, William Napier, would not hesitate to publish to the world the unscrupulous lengths to which those leaders were now prepared to carry their efforts. The trial of the leaders of the Irish physical-force party at Clonmel on a charge of high treason seemed to Sir William to be just the occasion he had threatened his correspondent with. That he held the letter we have described had long been an open secret, and it was therefore no wonder that he was summoned by the counsel conducting the prisoners' defence. Early in October, 1848, the appearance of this majestic veteran as a witness at the trial of Mr. Smith O'Brien fluttered the Whig dovecots from one end of the kingdom to the other. Of course there was the usual howl of execration from the whole tribe of self-styled loyalists, office-holders, highly-paid idlers, and others; but nevertheless William Napier was perfectly true to all the noble traditions of his race and his life in this action of his in behalf of a man who, though terribly mistaken in the line he had adopted, had been given only too much excuse for despairing of remedying the wrongs and miseries of his countrymen by any method of constitutional action.

It happened that in the same month which witnessed these proceedings in Clonmel a large public banquet was given to Charles Napier by the citizens of Dublin, and it was of course impossible that the action taken by one brother in opposition to the Whig Government should not have been made an occasion for trying to injure, if not prevent, the compliment about to be paid to the other brother in Dublin. Nothing could have been meaner and more ignoble than this attempt to step between the citizens of Dublin and the old soldier whom they wished to honour. The attempt failed, as it deserved to fail. The banquet was a splendid ovation. It was followed by another dinner at Limerick, where the entire people united to honour the guest of the citizens. During his stay in the Irish capital Napier visited the Theatre-Royal, and the whole house rose and gave him an enthusiastic welcome when he appeared at the front of the box. The heart of the man seemed deeply touched by these evidences of affection from the Irish people. "If I loved Ireland before, gratitude makes me love her more now," he writes. "My father and mother seemed to rise before my eyes to witness the feelings of Dublin towards me." This was indeed fame. Exactly fifty years earlier he had left the old city of Limerick to ride off to his life of war and wounds and wanderings, and through all the long intervening years he had never forgotten the land or the people of his boyhood. Now he was repaid. These ringing cheers and looks of welcome were the fittest answer to the impotent spleen of men in power who had denied him the just recognition of his labours and his victories. They had showered peerages and baronetcies upon the heads of the leaders of the incomplete Punjaub campaign. On the victor of Scinde only the most trifling rewards had been bestowed, and now the people, always just in their final verdict, had reversed the award.

Napier went for the last time to Celbridge. How strange it seems to him! How dwarfed it all is by the mighty battles through which the path of life has led him! The old scenes are there—the river, with its overhanging trees; the green fields, the fences, the terrace; the house where every window and door and wall holds some separate memory; the blue hill-tops along the southern horizon that used to be leagues distant, but now look close at hand, as though they had one and all shrunken in size. And so they have; because in after-life we look at each scene across many mounds, and a hundred beloved figures and faces of childhood rise up from the grave to dim our sight with tears.

Back to Cheltenham again to the war against Directors and their confederates, and to other work too. There are many veterans "wearing out the thread" in the town, and they love to come to the old hero and retail their woes to him. No sending out of a shilling to the door by footman or valet, but a talk over old times, and kind words as well as money to these old, worn-out stop-bullets. "Poor old fellows," he writes, "it vexes me to see them so hard run for small comforts, and I am glad I came here, if it were only for the chats with them of old fights and hardships. They like this, but complain bitterly that old officers take no notice of them. When I see these shrivelled old men with age ploughed deep in their wrinkled old faces like my own, and remember the deeds they did with the bayonet, I sigh for ancient days when our bodies were fit for war. I remember these men powerful and daring in battle, for they are mostly my own soldiers." With Napier there was no such thing as a "common soldier"; the man who went out and fought and marched and toiled was a hero—a private soldier hero if you will, but a hero all the same. The whole gorge of the man rose at the thought that the men who had bled for England should die in an English poorhouse; that there were thousands and tens of thousands who rolled in carriages, and drew dividends, and made long speeches in Parliament, and ate truffles and turtle, because these wizened old scarecrows had in days gone by charged home, or stood like stone walls under murderous storms of grape and musketry, or climbed some slippery breach amid the mangled bodies of their comrades.

A great victory over his numerous and powerful enemies at home was now in store for Charles Napier. Suddenly, while they were in the midst of their cabals and intrigues—pulling the thousand strings of mendacity which gold has ever at its disposal—the crash of disaster to our arms in India struck panic into the Directors and the Government. The Khalsa leader, Sheere Singh, had declared war in the northern Punjaub, and the Dhurum-Kha-Klosa, or religious war-drum of the Sikhs, was beating from Peshawur to the Chenaub. The Indian Government affected to treat this new Punjaub war as a trifling revolt. The price paid in life and treasure for the war that had ended not three years earlier had been so heavy, and the rewards given to the victors were so great, that this striking proof of incompleteness had to be minimised as much as possible. It was really nothing. Nobody need be alarmed. The Commander-in-Chief in India, Lord Gough, had ample force at his command to crush this partial uprising of the remnant of the Khalsa army. So said and wrote the Directors, and so said and wrote the many echoing speakers and scribes who enjoyed their patronage. All this went on during the early winter of 1848. Lord Gough, a brave and distinguished veteran of that type of soldier whose straight and simple code of honour made him unfitted to deal with the inherent mendacity of the Directorate, felt himself obliged to act up to the picture so plausibly painted by his civil superiors. They said he had sufficient force, and that the enemy was to be despised. In honour bound he must prove these statements to be true. The old fire-eater forgot that he was risking his army and his reputation for men who would be false to him at the slightest breath of adversity, and would unhesitatingly cast him overboard if by doing so they could prolong for even an hour their own truculent power. Gough advanced from an ill-stored base upon the enemy. After a most unfortunate encounter between our advanced troops and the Sikhs at Ramnugger, the English general crossed the Chenaub, and engaged the whole Khalsa army at Chillianwallah, on January 13th, 1849. In this memorable encounter disaster followed upon error, until night stopped the fighting. Infantry were moved up in close formation to masked batteries, no reconnaissance had been carried out, the positions of the Sikh army had to be found by the lines advancing to storm them, and the troops were formed up to fight their enemy after a long and fatiguing day's march when they should have been lying asleep in camp. When daylight dawned upon this scene of the confused fight of the previous evening, it was found that the Sikhs had fallen back, but we had lost above two thousand men, half of whom were Europeans; four guns and six standards had also been taken from us. British soldiers will fight their leaders through many scrapes and mistakes, but Chillianwallah had been too prolific in error to be saved even by heroism. When the news of this battle reached England, the entire nation cried out with one voice for Charles Napier at the helm of India, and of all the bitter draughts ever swallowed by any Honourable Company of Traders assuredly the bitterest was this forced acceptance as their Commander-in-Chief of the man whom now for six years they had been assailing in public and in private throughout the entire English empire. All honest England laughed loud at their discomfiture. Every real man welcomed with joy the triumph of the old hero over his treacherous and powerful foes. But a week before the news of this disaster Napier had been holding his own with difficulty against the enmity of Ministers, Directors, and the leading organs of the Press. The most persistent efforts had been made to confiscate his prize-money and to destroy his military reputation. Only a month earlier he had written to his brother, "I have always an idea of what you expect, viz. the Directors trumping up some accusation against me, but they can do nothing, because I have done nothing wrong." With all his knowledge of character he was still ignorant of the limits to which the hatred of a corporate body can extend. When Charles Napier was sent for by the Duke of Wellington, and offered, by order of the Queen, the command in India, that laconic but celebrated conversation took place. "If you don't go, I must," had said the Duke. There could only be one answer to this, and when next day the Press announced that Napier was to proceed at once to India as Commander-in-Chief, the whole voice of England ratified the appointment.

But the most striking moment of triumph had still to come. It was usual for the Directors of the Company to give a banquet to the man who was about to leave England to command the royal and the native armies. Napier accepted the invitation. The hatchet was to be buried. Salt was to be eaten. The old Duke was present. Some of the Ministers were there, but others were noticeable by their absence. It was a moment when a smaller mind than Napier's might easily have allowed itself the exultation of victory, but the old soldier spoke without trace of triumph. "I go to India," he said, "at the command of Her Majesty, by the recommendation of the Duke of Wellington, and I believe I go also with the approbation of my countrymen;" and then, without deigning to speak of the past and its contrast with the moment, he quietly observed, "Least said is soonest mended," thanked his hosts for their hospitality, and sat down.

Then there came a short and busy interval, in which what is called "the world" ran mad after the hero, not, indeed, because any more of a hero than he had been a month or a year or twenty years before, but simply because "the world" thought he could do it a good turn in the matter of its brothers and sons and nephews. The redoubtable "Dowb" had to be "taken care of" all along the line, and who can take care of him better than a Commander-in-Chief in India? One little item from that time should not be forgotten by those who want to know what manner of man this Charles Napier was. Just before starting for the East a sudden command reached him summoning him to dine at Osborne. He has no Court dress. There is a yellow or drab waistcoat, however, of old-world fashion and finery upon which he has set store for years. What could be nicer than this garment? They tell him that it is somewhat out of date—that it is too high in the collar or too long in the body; in fact, that it won't do. What is to be done? Only this. He has a valet—Nicholas by name, Frenchman and dandy—and this valet has a very fine waistcoat. So the waistcoat of Nicholas is produced, and off to the Isle of Wight goes the Commander-in-Chief to kiss the hand of the sovereign he has served so well. No man is a hero to his valet, says the proverb. We cannot say what Nicholas thought of his master; but this we can say, that among many soldier hearts throbbing for their Queen, Her Majesty had none more truly heroic than the old one that beat that day beneath the valet's waistcoat.

CHAPTER XIII
COMMANDER-IN-CHIEF IN INDIA

To India again, sixty-seven years old, and frequently suffering physical pain such as few men can know. Only a month before sailing he had thus described his sensations. "The injured nerves [of the face] carry inflammation up to the brain and it is not to be borne. I cannot tell what others may suffer, but they have not had the causes that affect me to affect them; they have not had the nerves torn by a jagged ball passing through, breaking nose-bones and jaw-bones, and lacerating nerves, muscles, and mucous membranes; they can hardly therefore have suffered as I do; if they have, their fortitude is beyond mine, for I cannot bear even the thought of it. It makes every nerve in my body tremble, even now, from writing on the subject."

On May 6th, 1849, Napier landed at Calcutta to find the Sikh War over. Lord Gough had completely vanquished the Khalsa arms at Goojerat, and resistance ceased from that day. Though perhaps in one sense this was a disappointment to Napier, he rejoiced that a fine old soldier should have been able by this victory to vindicate his military reputation. "It was hard," he writes, "that a brave old veteran like Gough, whose whole life has been devoted to his duty, should be dismissed from his command and close his long career under undeserved abuse, because the Directors kept him in a post that had become too difficult." But though actual hostilities had ceased there was work enough in India for a score of Commanders-in-Chief to set right. From top to bottom the whole administrative and executive system of the Indian army was wrong, and what was worse, was wrong from such a multiplicity of great and small causes that any attempt to set it right might well have appeared hopeless to the best administrative head ever set on the most vigorous body. There was no single point or no half-dozen points upon which the attempt at reform could be begun. It was not a passing distemper of the military body. It was dry rot and organic disease showing itself outwardly, indeed, in numerous symptoms of insubordination and lack of discipline; but the roots of which nothing but a gigantic incision could reach.

Leaving Calcutta in the end of May and proceeding by the slow methods of travel then in vogue, the new Commander-in-Chief reached Simla late in June. Here he met the Governor-General, Lord Dalhousie, and here in a few weeks began those strifes and contentions which eventually broke the old soldier's heart. Although the subjects of contention between the Commander-in-Chief and the Governor-General were many, and although all interest in them individually has long since evaporated in time, they still form, when viewed collectively in the light of the ever-to-be-remembered catastrophe of 1857, by far the most momentous reading that can be presented to-day to the statesman or the student of our empire. For the issue fought out by this soldier Chief and this civil Governor is yet before the nation, and some day or other will have to be decided, even in larger lists than that which witnessed its first great test in the Indian Mutiny of 1857.

War in a nation resembles a long and wasting disease in a human subject. It has a period of convalescence, when all the weak points of the system seem to threaten destruction even when the fever has passed. So it was in India now. Ever since 1838 war had been going on in India or close beyond its frontier. The Sikh War of 1849 ended the long catalogue, was in fact the last gust of the Afghan storm; but every administrative evil, civil and military, now lay exposed upon the weakened frame, and Napier's quick eye, long trained in the experience of Scinde, read almost at a glance the dangerous symptoms. Resolutely he bent himself to the thankless task of reform. He was Commander-in-Chief of a great army, but an army which had gone wholly wrong from the evil system which had crept into it from a hundred sources. He would trace out these sources of evil, cure them or cut them out, and leave India a record of his rule as Commander-in-Chief which would be of greater service to her than if he had led this army to the most brilliant victory. Such, in a few words, was the purpose he set himself to work for from the moment he set foot in India, and found that his task was not to be one of war.

Shortly after his arrival in Simla he began again to keep a journal, and in its pages we see, as in a mirror, the source of every outward act of his life traced out through every thought. In that journal the whole story of his effort and his failure, of the endless communings with those two great counsellors whom he long before declared should be the only prompters a man of action should have, "his conscience and his pillow," and of the difficulties and obstacles that met him at every step, is set forth. Here at Simla he sits, thinking and writing, collecting reports, reading despatches from every part of India, and writing down a vast mass of advice and recommendation, of warning and forecast, which, seven years later, are to seem like the prophecies of some inspired seer.

"The clouds are below us," he writes to his sister, "flying in all directions; and oftentimes, as one sits in a room, a cloud walks in as unconcernedly as a Christian, and then melts away." So, too, below him lay the thousand clouds of selfish struggle and petty contention which for ever seem to hover over our government of India; but, alas! when these clouds came up to Simla they did not melt away, but settled in a thickening gloom between him and the goal he strove so hard to reach. "I am working fifteen hours a day at my desk," he writes again, "working myself to death here; and what fame awaits me? None! I work because it is honest to earn my pay; but work is disagreeable in the extreme—hateful. Were I to remain five years I might do some good to this noble army; but for the short time I am to be here nothing can be done—at least nothing worth the loss of health and happiness. Never, however, did I know either, except when working in a garden or in Cephalonia making roads and doing good." And now, it may be asked by some persons, what were the reforms which this man endeavoured to effect? Why did he not leave well alone? Forty years have passed since Charles Napier "worked himself to death" at Simla, striving to set right the army and the military administration of India. He was thwarted in his labours, ridiculed for his fears, censured for his measures of reform. The men who opposed him became the petted favourites of his enemies. His own friends were marked out for enmity or neglect. He resigned. Time passed. The old soldier sank into his grave, and the hatred of his detractors did not ease its slander even when the tomb had closed upon the hero. Seven years went by, and suddenly the storm he had so vainly foretold broke upon India and upon England. The native army of Bengal mutinied. India ran with blood. Men, women, and children perished in thousands. Massacre and ruin overspread the land. Fortunately the blow fell when the nation, at peace with the great powers of the world, was able to concentrate all her energies upon India. But the struggle was a life-and-death one, and had Bombay and Madras followed the lead of Bengal, all was over. "Yes," I think I hear some one say, "but did not the Bengal army rise in revolt because greased cartridges were given to them with a new rifle?" My friend, the greased cartridge had to say to the Indian Mutiny just what pulling the trigger of a gun has to say to the loading of the charge. Long before ever a greased cartridge was heard of, the big gun of India had been loaded and rammed and primed and made ready to go off at the first hair-trigger's excuse it could find; and it was this loading and priming that Charles Napier was doing his utmost to draw from the gun during his tenure of Commander-in-Chiefship, and it was this loading and priming that his opponents were filling further and ramming harder by their ignorant opposition to him.

When the cool season begins, the Commander-in-Chief sets out upon his tour of inspection. How different it is from the triumphal progress heretofore usual! "What does an officer want in the field?" he had written shortly before leaving England; "his bed, his tent, a blanket, a second pair of breeches, a second pair of shoes, half a dozen shirts, a second flannel waistcoat, a couple of towels, and a piece of soap; all beyond is mere luxury, and not fit for a campaign." So, too, when the Commander-in-Chief was seen on his tour with diminished elephants and fewer camels and no bullocks, and only a third of the usual number of tent-pitchers and half the force or establishment of *chupprassees* and absolutely no *doolie-wallahs* at all, old Indians looked mutely at each other in speechless deprecation of such enormities. Then a thousand stories were circulated against the innovator. "He only gave claret at dinner to his guests; his tent was not big enough to swing a cat in; and because he had reduced the government *bheesties* (water-carriers) by half, it was clear he did not wash," etc., etc. But notwithstanding these criticisms and censures, the Commander-in-Chief went on from station to station, and never was examination so keen or inspection so close. Nothing escaped the eye that looked through these big spectacles. He is out at earliest dawn looking into matters in a regimental cantonment as closely as though he had been quartermaster-sergeant. One morning in some cantonment they miss him; he is not in the barracks nor on the parade-ground. The colonel gets nervous. "Go," he says to the adjutant, "go to the sergeant-major on the parade, and ask him if he has seen the Commander-in-Chief." But the sergeant-major is also missing; he is not on the parade. "Then ride over to his quarters and see if he is there." They go over to the staff-sergeant's quarters, and there sure enough is the missing sergeant-major, having a cup of tea and a bit of bread inside with a stranger. The nervous colonel becomes irate. The sergeant-major has no right to be in his quarters at such a critical time, when the most hawk-eyed Commander-in-Chief that ever held office is prowling about. "What are you doing in your quarters, sergeant-major?"—"The Commander-in-Chief is having some ration-bread and commissariat tea inside, sir," replies the sergeant-major, with a twinkle in his austere eye. And now out comes the missing Commander, face to face with the much-perplexed and puffed colonel. There is lightning in the eye behind the glasses. "And this is the bread your men are getting, sir," he says, holding out a half-eaten crust. "No wonder you have half your regiment in hospital."

At another station there is a young officer under arrest, awaiting the decision of the Commander-in-Chief upon his court-martial. He has been tried on a charge of having forgotten the respect due to his captain on a certain delicate occasion. The proofs were painfully clear; the young man had been convicted and sentenced to be cashiered. But there were many mitigating circumstances in the case; the officer was very young, and there was ample reason for supposing that the fruit he had stolen had not required much shaking. The Commander-in-Chief read the case carefully. "Sentence quashed," he wrote on the margin. "History records but one Joseph; this officer will return to his duty." These things, however, were but the play-moments of his progress; very serious matters soon claimed attention. In July, 1849, symptoms of mutiny began to manifest themselves in at least two regiments of Bengal Native Infantry stationed in the Punjaub. In November certain corps ordered to proceed to the Punjaub from Delhi openly showed insubordination. In December still graver signs of revolt occurred. The Thirty-Second Bengal Native Infantry refused to accept their pay, and mutinously demanded increased rates. The presence of a veteran general officer quelled this outbreak at Wuzzerabad, but a still more serious instance of insubordination was soon to manifest itself. In February, 1850, the Sixty-Sixth Regiment of Bengal Infantry broke into open mutiny at Govind Ghur, a suburb of Umritsur the sacred city of the Sikhs. The mutineers endeavoured to seize the fort, containing vast stores of arms and a large amount of treasure and ammunition. Again the vigorous action of an officer saved the gates, and a European regiment arriving in the nick of time overawed the rebellious Bengalees.

All these signs and portents of trouble were not lost upon the Commander-in-Chief; his resolution was quickly taken. By a stroke of the pen he disbanded the mutinous regiment, and put in its place a battalion of Ghoorka troops. The Governor-General was absent on a sea-voyage for the benefit of his health when this last alarming outbreak occurred at Umritsur. The case was urgent, the danger pressing. Twenty-four other Bengal regiments stationed in the Punjaub were known to be in close sympathy with the Sixty-Sixth; if the insubordination spread, the Sikh fires of resistance so lately quenched at Goojerat would again burst into flame. Gholab Singh was ready in Cashmere with a well-filled treasury and a large army to join the conflagration. The very existence of our Indian rule stood in peril. Napier was not the man to waste precious moments at such a crisis in seeking for precedents or covering his actions with the sanction of higher authority obtained by delay. He took three important steps.

Rightly judging that at such a moment any reduction of pay below the existing standard would give the discontent of the native troops a tangible and certain line of resistance, he directed that the promulgation of an order of the supreme Government, which would reduce the sepoys' allowances for rations below the standard then existing, and which had been originally framed chiefly to save the clerks in Calcutta trouble in their official documents, should be suspended, pending the result of a reference which would be made to the supreme Government on the subject. He next struck a crushing blow at the actual offenders in mutiny, by summarily disbanding the rebellious corps. And lastly he struck another vital blow at the entire Brahmin spirit of revolt, by enlisting Ghoorkas and putting them in the vacant places of the Bengalees, giving the new Ghoorka battalion the colours and number of the disbanded regiment.

Reviewing these lines of action now—even without the terrible after-light of the great Mutiny to guide our decision—it would be difficult for any sane man to find aught in them but ground for unqualified approval. They contain, indeed, such manifest evidences of sense and reason, that the man would appear to be bereft of the most elementary common sense who could find fault with them; and yet, incredible though it may well appear, not only was censure passed upon Napier for his action in this matter, but it was conveyed in such a rough and overbearing manner that the old soldier deemed it inconsistent with his honour to serve longer under such "shop-keeping" superiors. No other word can so fitly express the mental calibre of the men whose censure drove Charles Napier from the Indian command, and it is here used in a sense quite different from the usual caste acceptation of the term. The soldier and the shop-keeper must ever remain at opposite poles of thought. At their best, one goes out to fight for his country, and if necessary to die for it; the other remains at home to live, and to live well by it. At their worst, one acquires by force from the enemy, the other absorbs by fraud from his friends. But between the best and the worst there is a vast class of mental shop-keeping people who, although they do not keep any shops, are nevertheless always behind the counter, always asking themselves, "Will it pay?" always totting up a mental ledger, in which there is no double entry but only a single one of self. Nothing would be more delusive than to imagine this great class had any fixed limits of caste, rank, or profession. It may have been so once; it is not so now, nor has it been so for many generations. It reaches very high up the ladder now. It has titles, estates, coats-of-arms, moors, mountains, and the rest of it. It can be very prominent in both Houses of Parliament. But there is one thing it can never be, and that thing is a true soldier.

It can wear uniform and rise to high military rank, and have thousands of men serving under it, but for all that, we repeat, it can never be a real soldier—and the reason is simple, nowhere to be found more straightly stated than by a very deep thinker of our own time, who says: "I find this more and more true every day, that an infinitude of tenderness is the chief gift of all truly great men. It is sure to involve a relative intensity of disdain towards base things, and an appearance of sternness and arrogance in the eyes of all hard, stupid, and vulgar people, quite terrific to such if they are capable of terror, and hateful to them if they are capable of nothing higher than hatred." There we have the whole story of Napier and his antagonists. There we have the explanation of what Balzac meant when he wrote, "There is nothing so terrible as the vengeance of the shop-keeper." Throughout more than forty years of his fighting life, Charles Napier was exposed to that hatred and that vengeance. It could not have been otherwise. To be hated is often the price the hero must pay in life for the love his name is to gather round it after death.

One little gleam of soldier service came to brighten these last months of so-called command in India. It was an expedition through the Kohat Pass on the northern frontier. The tribe of Afridees, incensed at an order of the

Civil Government stopping their supply of salt, had risen, massacred a detachment of soldiers, and occupied the pass, cutting off the station of Kohat. Three days after the news of the disaster to the troops reached Napier, he had organised his column and was in march for Kohat. He fought his way through the pass, relieved the post, and fought his way back again. It was the last flicker of the flame which had begun forty-one years before in the march to Corunna. The last fighting item in the journal is suggestive of many thoughts. A young ensign had been shot in the pass, another officer was mortally wounded; forty years of war and death in the battlefield had not dulled the "infinitude of tenderness" in the old soldier's heart. "My God," he writes, "how hateful is war! yet better die gloriously like young Sitwell than as my dear John did in the agonies of cholera"; then recollecting that the true soldier has no more right to pick and choose the manner of his death than he has to pick and choose the manner of his life, he goes on: "Fool that I am, to think Sitwell's death the best! We know nothing. How can I know anything about it? It was the impulse of a fool to think one death better than another. Prepare to die bravely, and let death come in whatever form it pleases God to send him." So closes the military record. A little later he wrote again: "I shall now go to Oaklands [his home in Hampshire], and look at my father's sword, and think of the day he gave it into my young hands, and of the motto on a Spanish blade he had, 'Draw me not without cause; put me not up without honour.' I have not drawn his sword without cause, nor put it up without honour."

Charles Napier returned from his last fight at Kohat to find the reprimand of the Indian Government awaiting him. He at once resigned. He was quite prepared to stifle his personal feelings in the matter, but the sense of his powerlessness to remedy the evil he so plainly saw decided him. He would no longer remain accountable to the country for disaster he was helpless to prevent, exposed to a hundred secret shafts of his antagonists, and certain to find his old enemies, the Directors of Leadenhall Street, bitterly hostile to him, except when danger menaced their ill-gotten possession. He remembered also that fifty-two years earlier he had seen "that great and good soldier, Sir Ralph Abercrombie, resign command in Ireland because he could not agree with the civil government." Yes, he would resign. The Hampshire home looked pleasant from afar. What memories, what perfumes these garden-walks have for the tired toiler in life! What violet so sweet, what rose so thornless as those we see, looking back to some garden that has been, looking forward to one that can never be! Although Napier resigned his command in April he did not leave India until the following spring, having to await the arrival of his successor. The intervening months were not idly spent. To the latest moment of his stay he laboured to improve the army he loved so well, to instil into the officer higher ideals of duty and nobler purpose of life, and to improve the condition of the man in the ranks, who to him was now, as always, never "a common soldier." Feeling certain that the dreadful mortality then existing among the European troops in India resulted solely from the wretched barrack accommodation which the parsimony of the Government would only allow, he laboured incessantly to shame the Administration into more liberal and humane concession. Yet in this noble effort he was constantly thwarted. The height of his barrack-rooms was reduced, the materials for construction lessened. In vain he showed that sufficient cubic space meant thousands of lives annually saved, that height of the sleeping-rooms above the ground meant freedom from fevers and dysenteries. The various Boards of Control and clerks in Calcutta were not to be moved by such considerations. Terrible examples were before these various Boards and Directorates, but still they were not to be convinced. After the battles of the Sutlej the remains of a splendid regiment, the Fiftieth, were sent to occupy one of these ill-built death-traps at Loodiana. In one fell night the entire building collapsed, and three hundred men, women, and children perished in the ruins. Of course it was nobody's fault. The regulations had been strictly adhered to—and does not everybody know that regulation is infallible? Did they not once let a king of Spain burn to death in his palace because the regulation extinguisher of royal fires was not present at the conflagration?

In the autumn of 1850 Charles Napier set out on the homeward journey. The last scenes in India were pleasant to the old soldier about to close his long and eventful career. He reviews once more his own favourite Twenty-Second Regiment and presents them with new colours. The soldiers of Meanee and Hyderabad received their chief with a frantic enthusiasm and delight that more than made amends for the neglect of the great and powerful; and the entire army too, whose deep heart the follies and the fashions of the moment cannot reach, bent its head as the old hero passed; and whatever was honest and independent and noble—and there was plenty of each in the Civil Service of India—laid its tribute of respect in his path, until from Simla to Scinde and on to Bombay the long sun of his military life seemed to be setting in waves of glory. But the tribute of honour that touched him deepest was a magnificent sword which the sirdars and chiefs of Scinde presented to him at Hyderabad. Nearly eight years earlier these men had fought against Napier at Meanee and Dubba. He had honoured their bravery in the hour of their misfortune. Now about to quit, under a cloud of official censure everywhere made public, the scene of his toil and glory, they, his old enemies, came to lay at his feet this token of their admiration.

CHAPTER XIV
HOME—LAST ILLNESS—DEATH

In March, 1851, Napier reached England. Many times, returning from some scene of war or foreign service, had he seen the white cliffs rise out of the blue waves. This was to be his last arrival, and perhaps it was the saddest in all his life. "I retire with a reprimand," he had said a few months earlier; and although he tried hard to keep in view the fact that in circumstances of sudden and grave danger to the State he had acted firmly, courageously, honestly, and with absolute sense and wisdom in every step he had taken, still all that only served to drive deeper into his injustice-hating heart the sting of unmerited and unjust censure.

He came home to die. Not all at once, indeed, did the end come. Such gnarled old oaks do not wither of a sudden, no matter how rude may be the shock; but the iron had entered into his soul, and the months of life that still remained were to be chiefly passed in pain and suffering. At first, after his arrival, business took him to London, and the long-dreamt-of happy gardening-ground in Hampshire was denied him. All through life he had hated the great city. "To be in London is to be a beast—a harnessed and driven beast—and nothing more," he writes. Neither its dinners nor its compliments nor its "pompous insolence" had ever given him the least concern. Like another great soldier who, in this year, 1851, was about to begin that military career which was to render his name so famous, Charles Napier had a contempt for the capital of his country. When the Directors of the East India Company had been on their knees to him, and the Lord Mayor and the rest of the great dining dignitaries had been begging his attendance at their banquets during the Punjaub disasters, he had not been in the least elated; and neither now was he depressed by their studied neglect of him when danger had passed by. "I never was in spirits at a London party," he writes, "since I came out of my teens."

In April he gets away to Oaklands, and prepares to settle down to the repose of a country life. "At last a house of mine own," he says. "All my life I have longed for this." But scarcely is he at home ere the disease, contracted in Scinde, increased in India, and aggravated by the ill-usage of the past year, brings him to the verge of death. He rallies again, but his thoughts are now set upon the great leave-taking. In his journal we seem to see him all the clearer as the end approaches. "When I die may the poor regret me," he writes; "if they do, their judgment will be more in my favour than anything else. My pride and happiness through life has been that the soldiers loved me.... I treated every soldier as my friend and comrade, whatever his rank was." What a contempt he has for the upstart in uniform, the martinet, the thing with the drawl and eyeglass! "As military knowledge decays, aristocratic, or rather upstart arrogance, increases," he writes. "A man of high breeding is hand and glove with his men, while the son of your millionaire hardly speaks to a soldier." Then he turns to the "coming world and all those I hope to meet there—Alexander, Hannibal, Cæsar, Napoleon, and my father." But the long-looked-for peace of life in the country—the garden, the pets, and the rest of it—is not to be. He has a beautiful Pyrenean dog, Pastor by name. A neighbouring farmer wantonly shoots this noble animal. Napier tries to punish the man at law. The case is clear against the dog-killer, but the local jury acquits him in spite of judge and evidence. "Trial by jury is a farce," we read in the journal. "Why, if Goslin [the dog-killer] had murdered his wife and child, they [the jury] could not have treated him more gently!"

Then come other worries of a more serious character. The East India Directors are doing all that wealth and power can do to take from him his Scinde prize-money. He was not the Commander-in-Chief of the army, they say, with a monstrous effrontery; and of course they have anonymous scribblers everywhere at work to blacken and defame their enemy. So, between the local numskull murdering his pet dogs and the cosmopolitan master-shop-keeper vilifying his character, the last months of the old soldier's life are vexed and unhappy.

Still, as the end draws nearer many bright gleams of sunshine come to gladden the old man's heart. Not only is the great heart of the nation with him, but all the kings of thought are on his side too. When the great Duke passes to his rest no figure in the throng of war-worn veterans around the coffin was so eagerly sought for as that of the man who, forty-two years earlier, had waved his hat to Lord Wellington when, unable to speak as he was carried desperately wounded from the fierce fight at Busaco, he thought this mute farewell was to be a last adieu. Men noted too with inward sense of satisfaction at the scene in St. Paul's that "the eagle face and bold strong eye" of the veteran who stood by the dead Duke's bier gave promise that England had a great war-leader still left to her.

But the "eagle face and the bold strong eye" were only those echoes of bygone life which are said to be strong as the shadows gather. And the shadows were gathering fast now. In June, 1853, the illness that was to prove mortal began. Still, we find him writing letters to help some old soldier who had served him in Scinde, and in the very last letter that he seems ever to have written, the names of Sergeant Power and Privates Burke and Maloney stand witness to the love for the private soldier which this heroic heart carried to the very verge of the grave. In July he was brought to Oaklands, as he wished that the end should come to him in his own home. There, stretched upon a little camp-bed in a room on the ground-floor of the house, he waited for death. It came with those slow hours of pain and suffering which so frequently mark the passing away of those in whom the spirit of life has been strong, and who have fought death so often that he seems afraid to approach and seize such tough antagonists. Frequently during the weeks of illness the old instincts would assert themselves in the sufferer. He would ask his veteran brother to defend his memory when he was gone, from the attacks of his enemies; or he would send messages through his son-in-law to the "poor soldiers," to tell them how he had loved them; and once he asked that his favourite charger, Red Rover—the horse that had carried him through the storm of battle at Meanee—might be brought to the bedside, so that for a last time he might speak a word to and caress the animal; but the poor beast seemed to realise the mortal danger of his old master, and shrank startled from the sick couch. As the month of August drew to a close it was evident to those who lovingly watched beside the sufferer that the end was close at hand. It came on the early morning of the 29th. The full light of the summer morning was streaming into the room, lighting up the shields, swords, and standards of Eastern fight which hung upon the walls; the old colours of the Twenty-Second, rent and torn by shot, moved gently in the air, fresh with the perfume of the ripened summer; wife, children, brothers, servants, and two veteran soldiers who had stood behind him in battle, watched— some praying, some weeping, some immovable and fixed in their sorrow— the final dissolution; and just as the heroic spirit passed to Him who had sent it upon earth, filled with so many noble aspirations and generous sympathies, a brave man who stood near caught the flags of the Twenty-Second Regiment from their resting-place and waved these shattered emblems of battle above the dying soldier. So closed the life of Charles Napier. When a great soldier who had carried the arms of Rome into remotest regions lay dying in the imperial city, the historian Tacitus tells us that "in the last glimpse of light" the hero "looked with an asking eye for something that was absent." Not so with Napier. Those he had loved so devotedly, those who had fought around him so bravely, those who had shielded his name in life from the malice of enemies, and who were still to do battle for him when he was in the grave—all these loving, true, and faithful figures met his last look on earth.

They laid Charles Napier beneath the grass of the old garrison graveyard in Portsmouth, for the dull resentment of oligarchic faction is strongest in the death of heroes, and a studied silence closed the doors of the two great cathedrals of the capital against ashes which would have honoured even the roll of the mighty dead who sleep within these hallowed precincts. Faction, for the moment dressed in power, forgot that by neglecting to place the body of Charles Napier with his peers, it was only insulting the dust of ten centuries of English heroism; and yet even in this neglect the animosity of power misplaced was but able to effect its own discomfiture, for Napier sleeps in death as he lived in life—among the brave and humble soldiers he had loved to lead; and neither lofty dome nor glory of Gothic cathedral could fitter hold his ashes than the narrow grave beside the shore where the foot of Nelson last touched the soil of England.

It was on September 8th, 1853, that the funeral took place at Portsmouth. Sixty thousand people—and all the soldiers who could come from miles around, not marching as a matter of duty, but flocking of their own accord and at their own expense to do honour to their dead comrade—followed the procession in reverent silence. Well might the soldiers of England mourn, not indeed for the leader but for themselves. Little more than one year had to pass ere these Linesmen, these Highlanders, these Riflemen, and twenty thousand of their brethren, lions though they were, would be dying like sheep on the plateau before Sebastopol—dying for the want of some real leader of men to think for them, to strive for them, to lead them. Two years later to a day, on September 8th, 1855, men looking gloomily at the Russian Redan and its baffled assailants might well remember "the eagle face and bold strong eye" and vainly long for one hour of Meanee's leading.

Nations, no matter how powerful, cannot afford to ill-use or neglect their heroes, for punishment follows swiftly such neglect, and falls where least expected. In an old Irish manuscript that has but lately seen the light, there is given in a few terse words a definition of the attributes of character which go to form a leader of men. "Five things," says this quaint chronicle, "are required in a general. Knowledge, Valour, Foresight, Authoritie, and Fortune. He that is not endowed for all or for most of these virtues is not to be reputed fit for his charge. Nor can this glory be purchased but by practice and proof; for the greatest fencer is not always the best fighter, nor the fairest tilter the ablest soldier, nor the primest favourite in court the fittest commander in camp." How aptly this description of a leader fits Charles Napier the reader can best judge. Knowledge, Valour, and Foresight he possessed to an extraordinary degree. Authority, so pertinaciously denied him by his chiefs, he asserted over men without the smallest difficulty. Fortune in the field was also largely his. How hard he practised to perfect all these gifts, and how repeated was their proof, no one who has read his life will venture to deny. But Charles Napier was many other things besides a great general. He had a hundred gifts and graces of character that must have made him famous in any sphere of life he had selected, and made him famous, not by the passive assent given by his fellows to his possession of some local eminence of character showing large amid the level of their own mediocrity, but by the sheer force of the genius that was in him, the flame of which was certain to force its way to the surface, despite all the efforts of envy to keep it down. Never lived there soldier who had so little greatness thrust upon him. From the day he began his military career to the moment he hung up his father's sword at Oaklands he had to win every grade and every honour three times over. He seemed, indeed, to delight in the consciousness that he possessed this triple power of conquest. Do what they would to deny him, he would go out again and force them to acknowledge him. And it was this inward consciousness of power that made him despise the trappings of rank or position which other men held so high. Like his great ancestor, Henry of Navarre, he laughed at pomp and parade. "Pomp, parade, and severe gravity of expression," said the great Bourbon, "belong to those who feel that without them they would have nothing that would impress respect. By the grace of God I have in myself that which makes me think I am worthy of being a king." So, too, like the Béarnois, Napier grounded his greatness deep down in the welfare of the peasant, in his love for them, and in the first prerogative of true leadership, the right of thinking and toiling for the benefit of the poor and humble. "My predecessors thought themselves dishonoured by knowing the value of a teston," Henry used to say. "I am anxious to know the value of half a denier, and what difficulty the poor have to get it. For I want all my subjects to have a fowl in the pot every Sunday." So was it with this soldier who was sixth in descent from the first Bourbon, and who fought so hard to keep the last on a throne his race would never have forfeited had they but remembered this golden rule of all true kingship.

Two things Napier carried through life of infinite importance—memory of home and hero-worship. He moved through life between these two lode-stones. The noble independence of mind possessed by his father, the ocean of love and tenderness of his mother, the associations of his early home, these were ever present through the wildest and roughest scenes of life—hallowed memories, green spots that deserts could not wither, nor fiercest fighting destroy. And in front lay the lofty ideal, the noble aspiration. Alexander, Hannibal, Cæsar, Napoleon—from early manhood these names were magnets to lift his mind above low desires and sordid cares, and when the shadows of death were gathering they still stood as lofty lights above the insults and the injustice of his enemies.

Carious too is it to watch in the career of Charles Napier how, out of the garden of memory which he kept green in his heart, many flowers sprang up as time went on, how his faith in an all-wise Providence strengthened and increased, how life beyond the grave became a positive necessity to him, how he looked forward to the time when men will think only of "acting right in the eyes of God, for then Christ will rule the world. What result will follow this utter defeat of the evil spirit, the God in heaven only knows, but the work will be Christ's work, and He will perhaps come to rule us with eternal life and happiness for those who have adhered to the Good Spirit—the God, who will then direct all things to His will." So must it ever be with the truly great minds which are based on what Mr. Ruskin calls "an infinitude of tenderness." They no more can live without religion than an oak-tree can grow without the sun. The mushroom, and the fungi, and the orchid of the human species may indeed flourish in the night of denial, but the hero is as certain to believe in God as the eagle is to seek the mountain-top.

Great lives have two lessons—one for the class to which the life belonged, the other to the nation which gave it birth. The latter is the lesson of paramount importance; for as the past is ever a mirror held up to the present in which to read the future, so the life of a dead hero may be said to mark for statesmen and rulers the rocks and shallows of their system of government. Never perhaps did a nation pay more swiftly and to the full the penalty of being blind to the real nature of the son which had been born to her than did England in her neglect of Napier. There are those who, writing and speaking of him since his death, have regretted his "utterances of passion," his "combativeness," his want of "serenity." "They [Charles Napier and his brother William] lived in storm instead of above the clouds," wrote one of their greatest admirers when both brothers had passed away; and if this has been said since they have left us, a hundredfold stronger was the censure of the world when they still moved among their fellow-men. But the passion and the vehemence of the Napiers was only the ocean wave of their hatred of oppression thundering against the bulwarks of tyranny. They should have dwelt above the clouds, forsooth, made less noise, toned down the vehemence of their denunciation. How easy all this is after the battle is over, and when we are sitting in a cushioned chair with our feet to the fire! But find me anything overthrown without noise, my friend—any citadel of human wrong captured, any battle ever won by the above-the-cloud method,—and I'll say you are right about these Napiers. Summer lightning is a very pretty thing, but lightning that has thunder behind it is something more than pretty. But perhaps I am wrong. They tell us now that battles are in future to be silent affairs—powder is to make no smoke, rifles and artillery are to go off without noise; there is to be no "vehemence" or "passion" about anything; you are to turn a noiseless wheel and the whole thing will be quietly done. All this is very nice, but I have an idea that when our sapient scientific soldier has arrived at all this noiseless excellence he will be inclined to follow the example of his rifle, and go off himself, making as little noise as possible in the operation, but in a direction opposite to his gun. So, being doubtful as to this question of noise, I turn to Charles Napier once more, and strangely enough this is what I read: "The rifle perfected will ring the knell of British superiority.

The *charging shouts* of England's athletic soldiers will no longer be heard. Who will gain by this new order of fighting? Certainly the most numerous infantry. The soldier will think how he can hide himself from his enemy instead of how to drive a bayonet into that enemy's body."[5]

One other point ere my task is done. The present is pre-eminently the age when men long most to ring the coin of success, and hear it jingle during life. People will say of Napier that he stood in his own light. It is true he told the truth, but look what it cost him. Had he kept silence he would have been made a peer; they would have buried him in St. Paul's or Westminster Abbey, and put a grand monument over his grave. Hearing which and thinking upon it one comes to ask a simple question,—What is success? As the world translates the phrase, Napier was perhaps not a successful man. Yet he lived to see the principles he had struggled for through life, and suffered for in his struggles, everywhere triumphant. The great circle of human sympathy growing wider with every hour, and some new tribe among the toiling outcasts of men taken within its long-closed limits. He lived to see a Greater Britain and a larger Ireland growing beyond the seas—fulfilling, in regions never dreamt of by Canning, the work of liberty and progress which that Minister had vainly imagined was to be the mission of the South American Republics.

And, coming from the great field of human justice and human liberty, in which he had ever been a manful fighter, to the narrower battle-ground of his own personal strifes and contentions, he lived, not indeed to see the truth of his opinions and the justice of his conduct fully vindicated by the unerring hand of Time, but near enough to the hour of that vindication to behold its dawn already reddening the horizon. When the light was made manifest to the world four years after the hero's death, the man who had stood faithful sentinel through so many years over his brother's fame— William Napier—was still left to hail the full-risen beam, and to show to a careless world the length and breadth of that signal vindication. And long before the lower crowd could see the light, it had flashed upon the great solitary summits. "A lynx-eyed, fiery man, with the spirit of an old knight in him," wrote Carlyle, one year before the Indian Mutiny. "More of a hero than any modern I have seen for a long time; a singular veracity one finds in him, not in his words alone, but in his actions, judgments, aims, in all that he thinks, and does, and says, which indeed I have observed is the root of all greatness or real worth in human creatures, and properly the first, and also the earliest, attribute of what we call *genius* among men." And then comes a bit which it would be well to write very high and very large in all the schools and examination rooms in the land. "The path of such a man through the foul jungle of this world, the struggle of Heaven's inspiration against the terrestrial fooleries, cupidities, and cowardices, cannot be other than tragical, but the man does tear out a bit of way for himself too; strives towards the good goal, inflexibly persistent, till his long rest come. The man does leave his mark behind him, ineffaceable, beneficent to all; maleficent to none. Anarchic stupidity is wide as the night; victorious wisdom is but as a lamp in it, shining here and there."

So wrote of Charles Napier the greatest thinker of our age—that is the mountain-top. If you want to find the other extreme of estimate, you will go to Trafalgar Square, and on the pedestal of Napier's statue there read— "Erected by Public Subscription, the most numerous Contributors being Private Soldiers." Between these two grades of admiration lies the life of Charles James Napier.

Printed by R. & R. CLARK, *Edinburgh*.

FOOTNOTE:

[5] *Defects of Indian Government.*